OUT of SQUARE

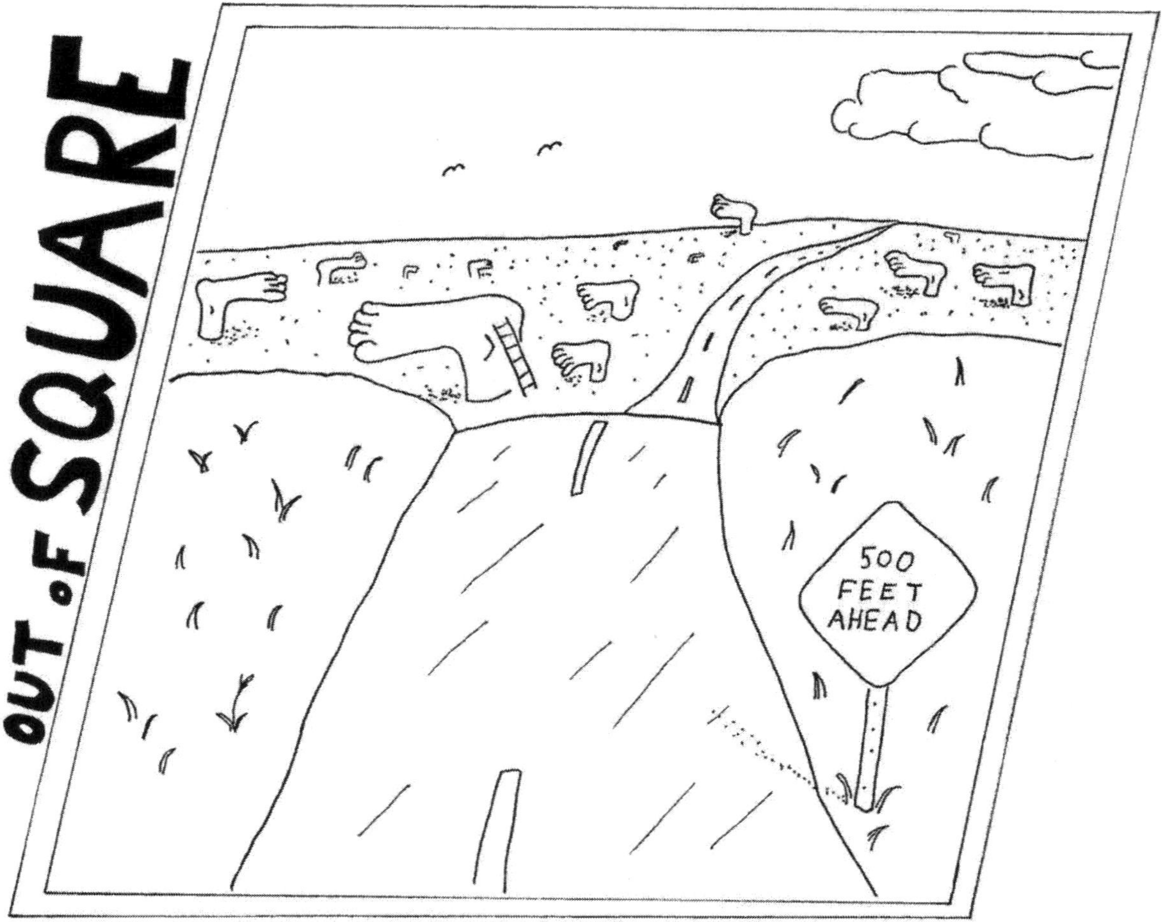
500
FEET
AHEAD

BY MATTHEW THERIAULT

Dedication:

The two people in my life that made this book possible; my father Gerald Earl Theriault for giving me his sense of humor and my wife Sherrie Rainey Theriault for loving it.

out of square

by Matthew Theriault

I was raised in a little farm north of Princeton NJ, and it served as a giant playground for me. My parents were fun and liberal. Connected to the Princeton UU church I had lots of academic family friends and was exposed to the newest of sciences. I think from the start I saw the world differently than my peers and teachers. Rules seem to hold little value and I saw the foolishness of much of the education process. I received an average mark in 9th grade art, which prevented me from continuing art education in high school. I look back on it now and realize it taught me "I was not an artist." Maybe they were right. I focused on the sciences and had a knack for electronics. Once I started work in manufacturing, I have stayed employed in the same company for more than 31 years now. Married with a son, we made a home in Warren County NJ and there Sherrie and I grew ourselves whole, together.

In the early 90's I took a pen and paper recording my observations about life. Mostly I started placing a drawing board between me and the cathode ray tube of the evening television sitcoms and melodramas. I wanted to see if I could envision an idea and draw a cartoon everyday much like a syndicated cartoonist. I believe those folks that are syndicated tend to produce many ideas a day and some are rejected. I wanted to know if I could create one funny idea even when I had the flu, the pipes in the house froze, and my dog had run away from home. I ended up creating nearly 90 different cartoons and for some reason the flow of new ideas just stopped. Ideas come from time to time and I wonder if I should continue to nurture the thinking and drawing. Sometimes life gets in the way of these endeavors.

These drawings have been parked for years not knowing what to do with them. So Sherrie combined them into a book with hopes others could enjoy them.
These funny ideas are all around us and I believe without living and experiencing life it's hard to envision these views. It is all about getting folks to laugh. Laughter is my family tradition, a medicine, a conveyer of a political point, and a lesson learned without experts.

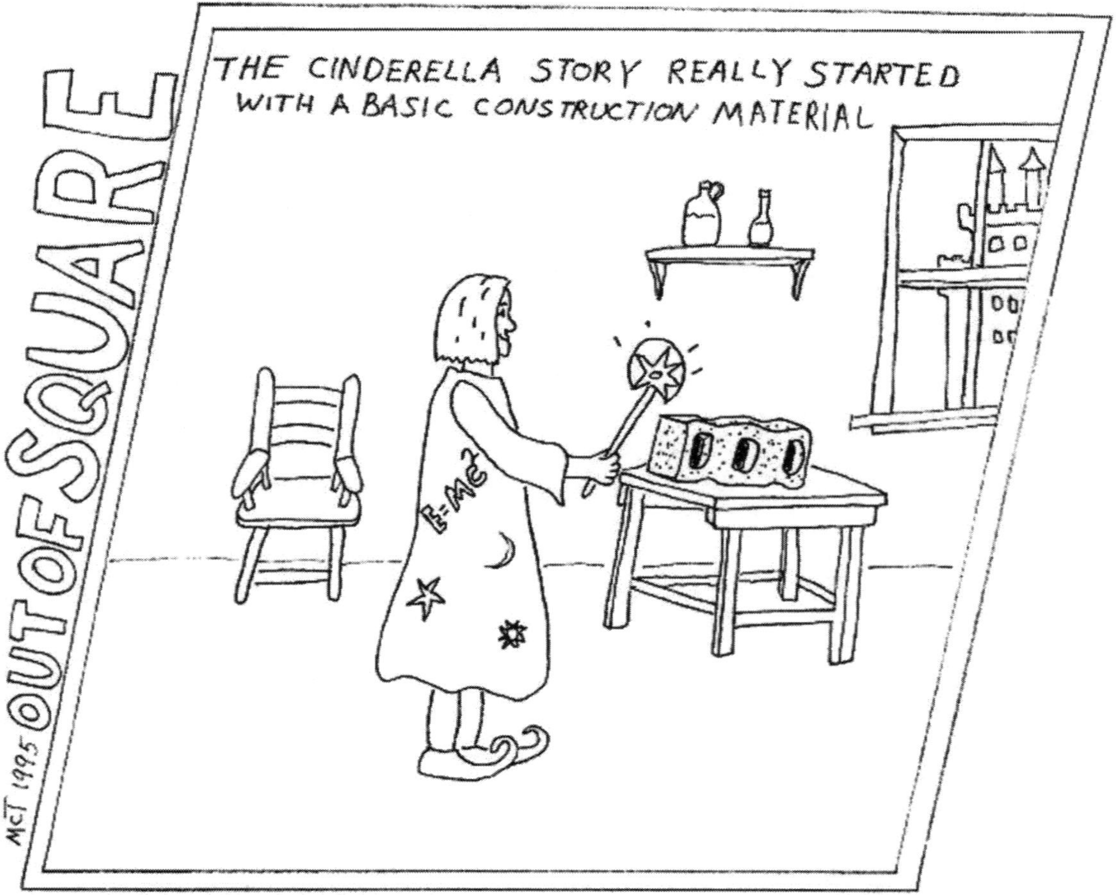
THE CINDERELLA STORY REALLY STARTED WITH A BASIC CONSTRUCTION MATERIAL
OUT OF SQUARE
McT 1995
E=MC²

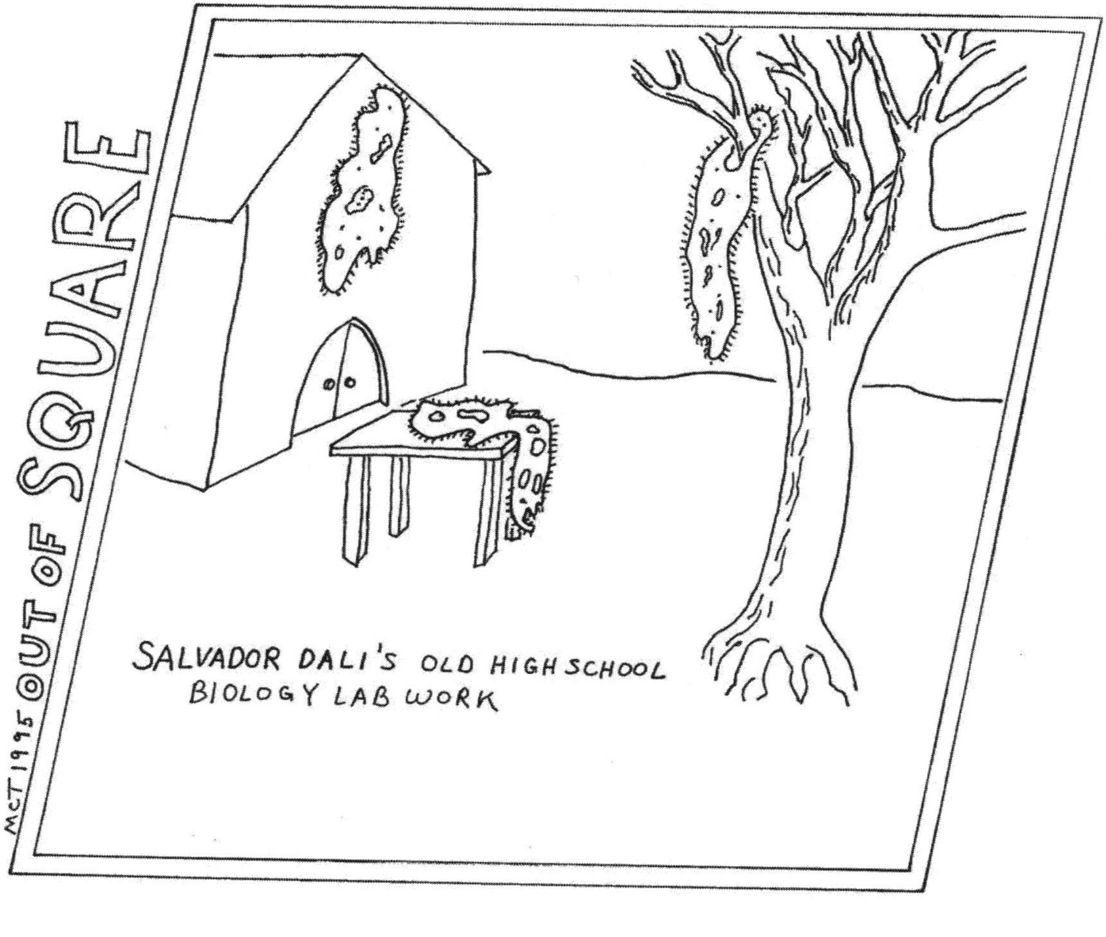
McT 1995 OUT OF SQUARE
SALVADOR DALI'S OLD HIGH SCHOOL
BIOLOGY LAB WORK

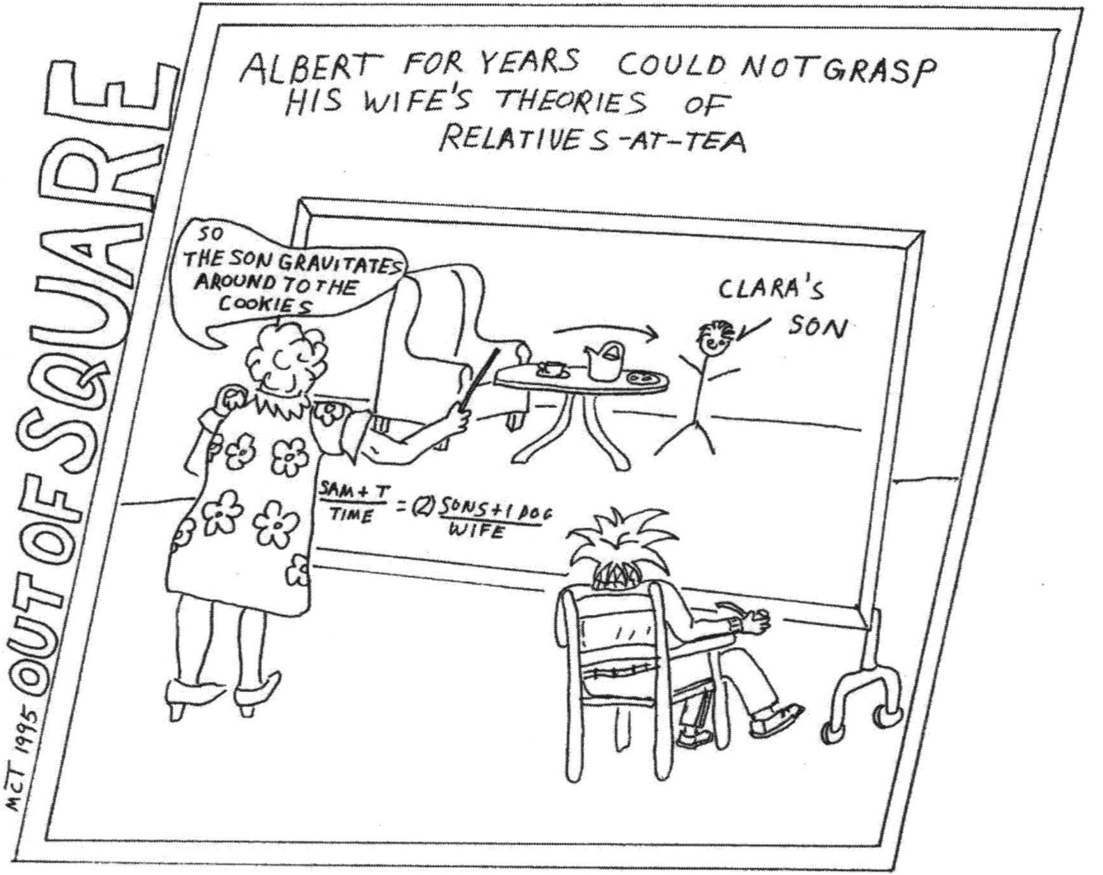
OUT OF SQUARE
MCT 1995
ALBERT FOR YEARS COULD NOT GRASP HIS WIFE'S THEORIES OF RELATIVES-AT-TEA
SO THE SON GRAVITATES AROUND TO THE COOKIES
CLARA'S SON
SAM + T / TIME = (2) SONS + 1 DOG / WIFE

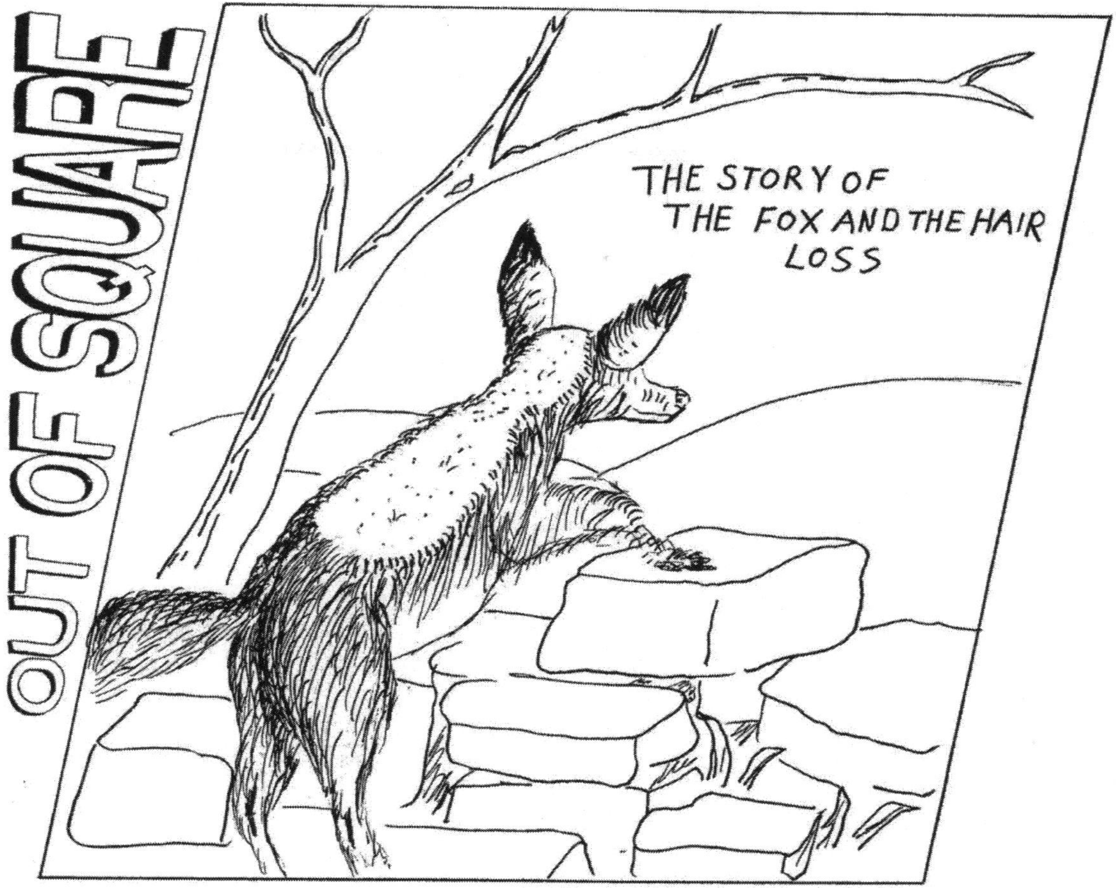
OUT OF SQUARE
THE STORY OF
THE FOX AND THE HAIR
LOSS

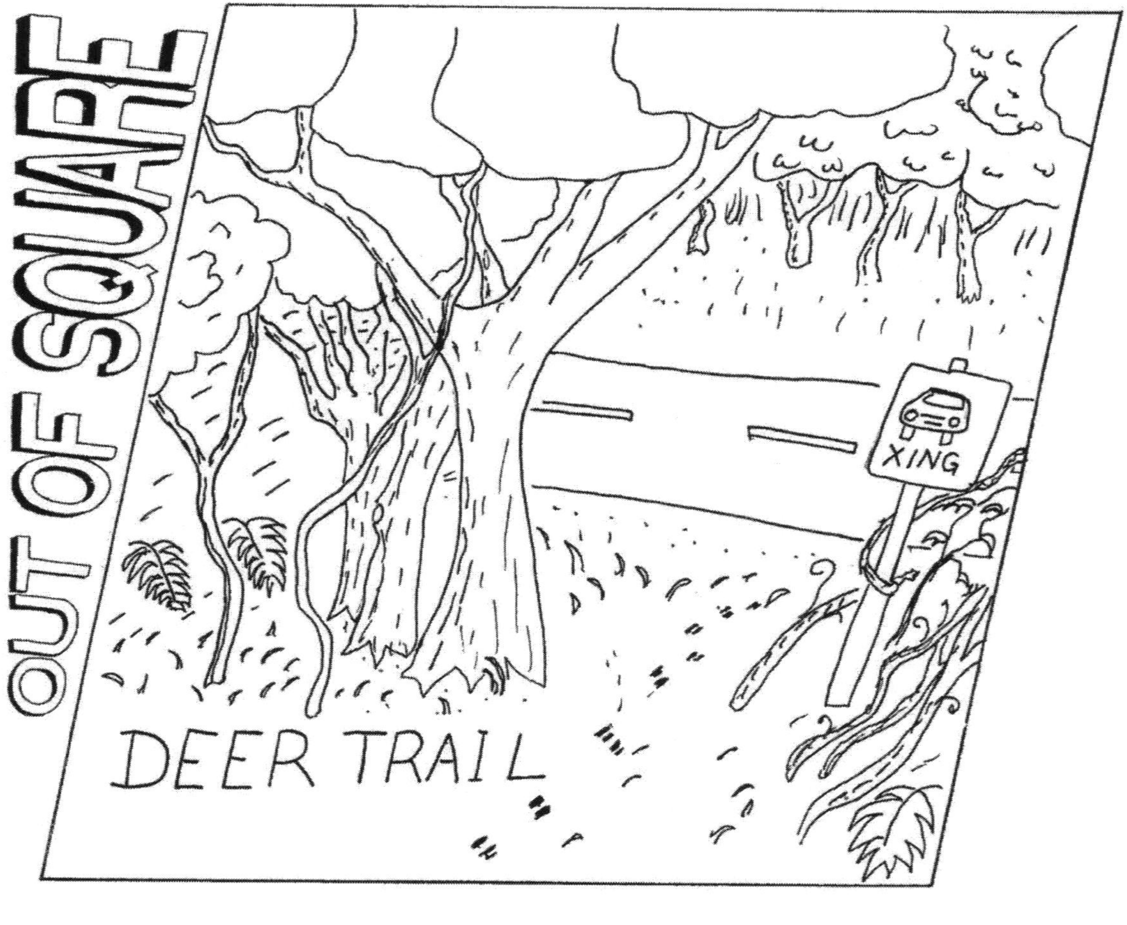
OUT OF SQUARE
DEER TRAIL
XING

OUT OF SQUARE

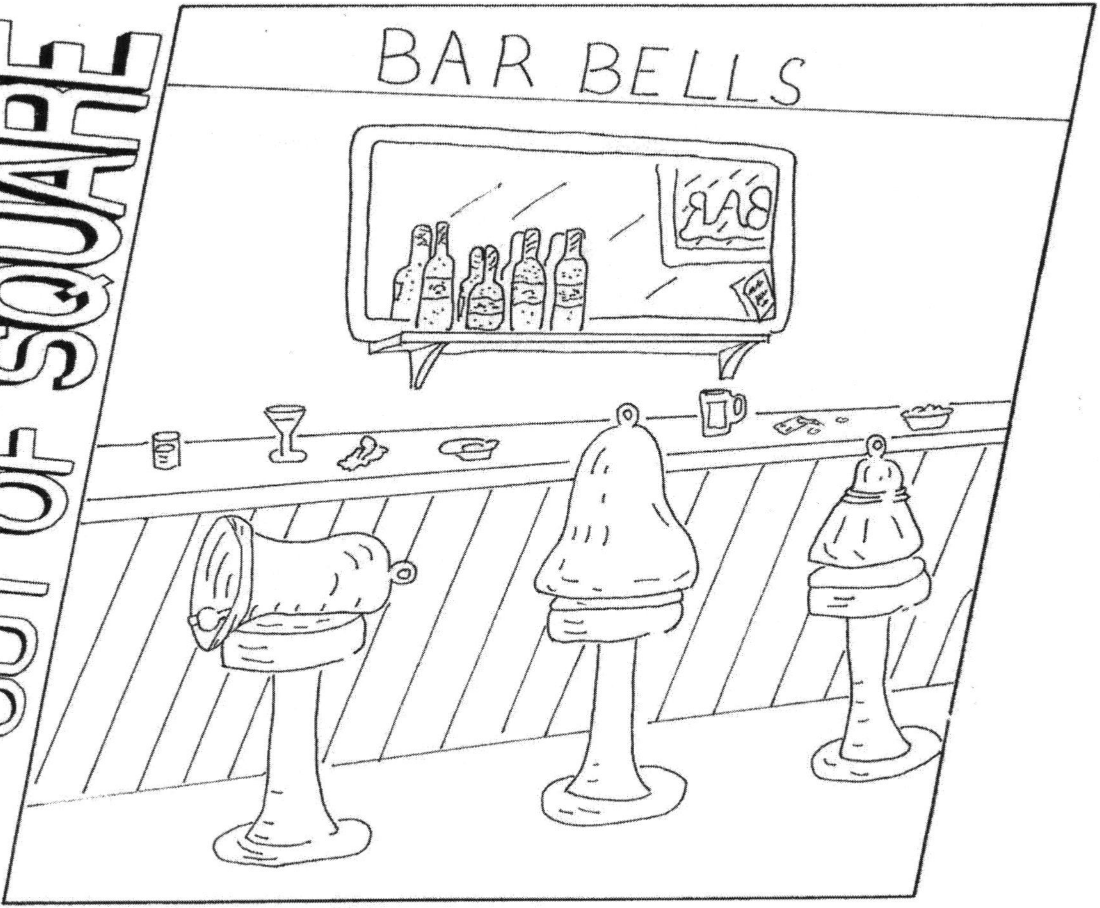
BAR BELLS

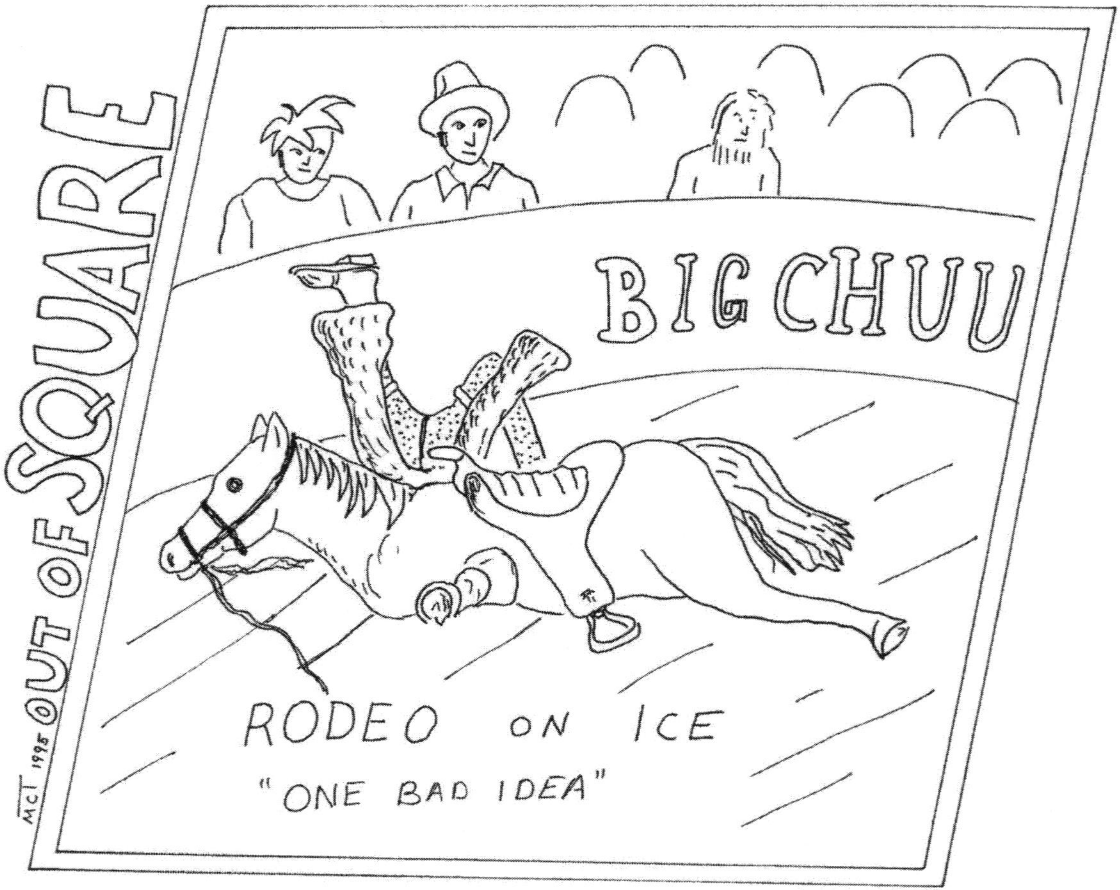
OUT OF SQUARE
MCT 1995
BIG CHUU
RODEO ON ICE
"ONE BAD IDEA"

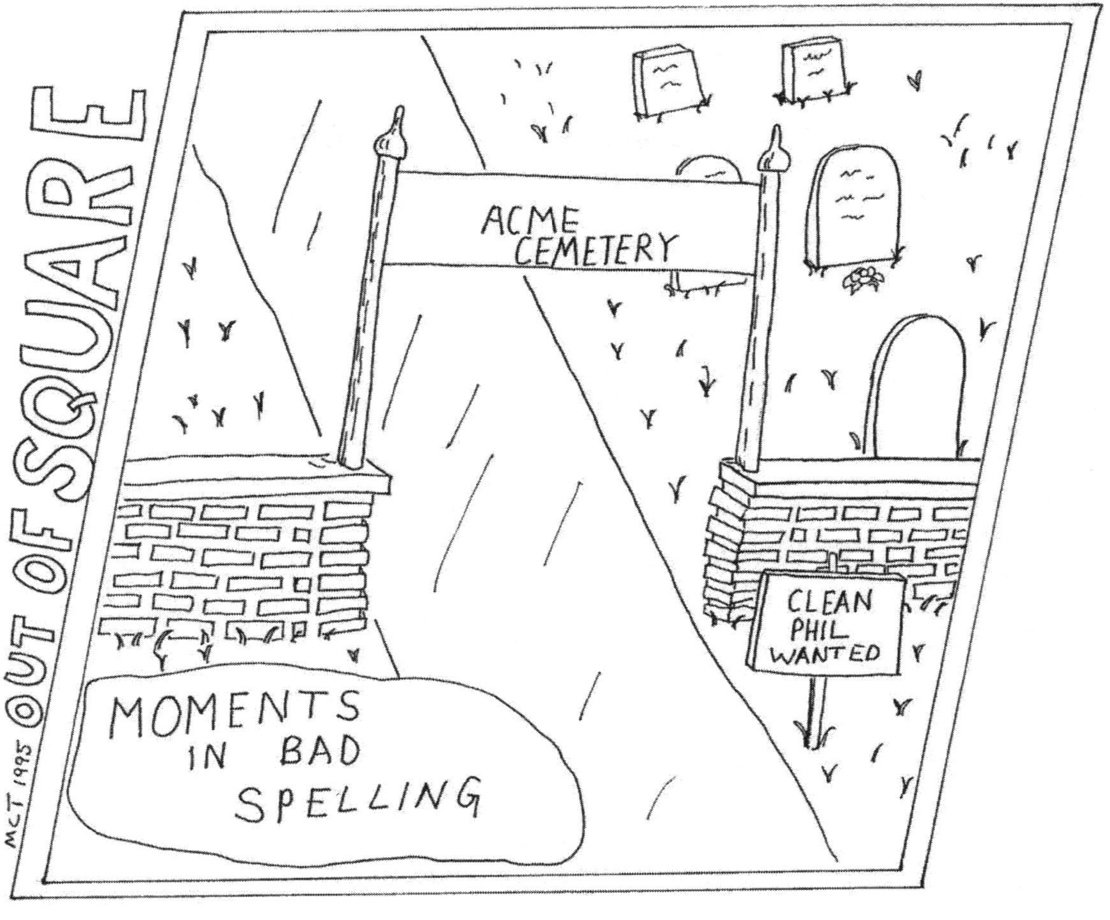
OUT OF SQUARE
MCT 1995
ACME CEMETERY
CLEAN PHIL WANTED
MOMENTS IN BAD SPELLING

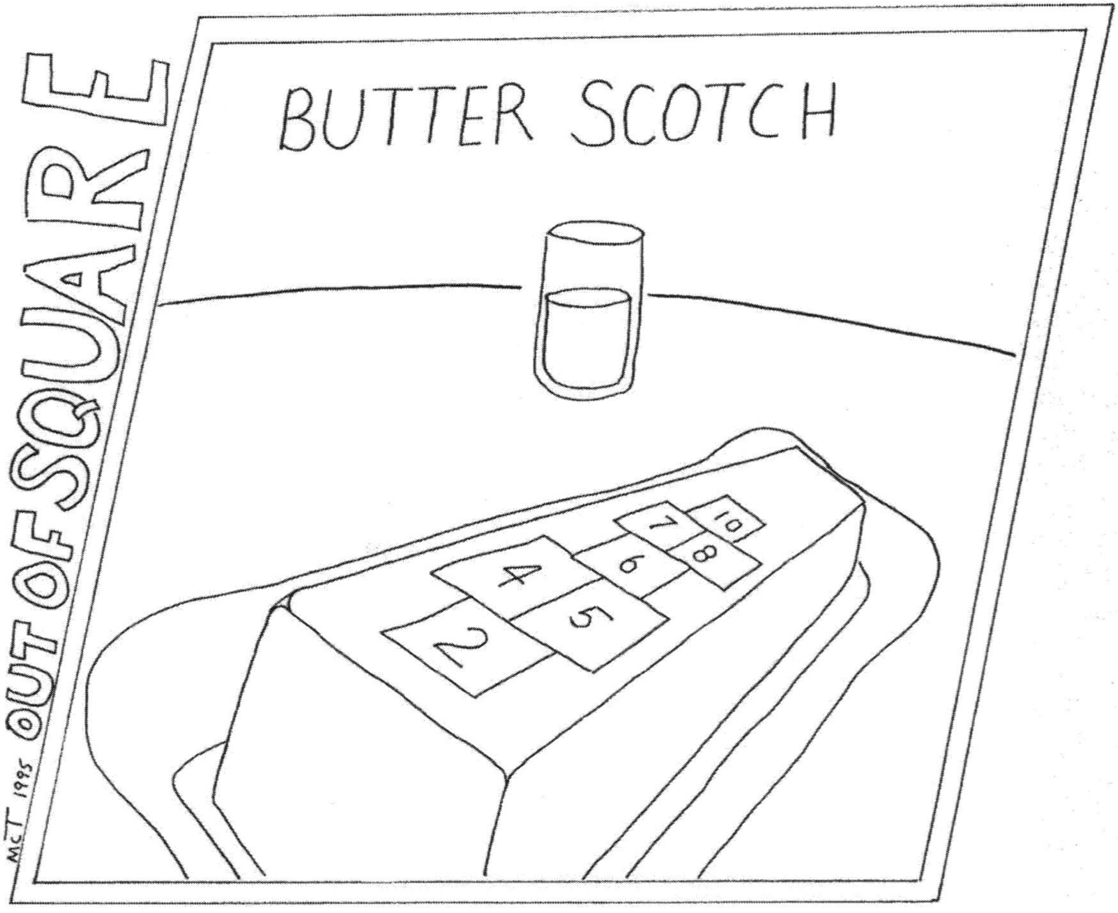
OUT OF SQUARE
MCT 1995
BUTTER SCOTCH
2
4
5
6
7
8
10

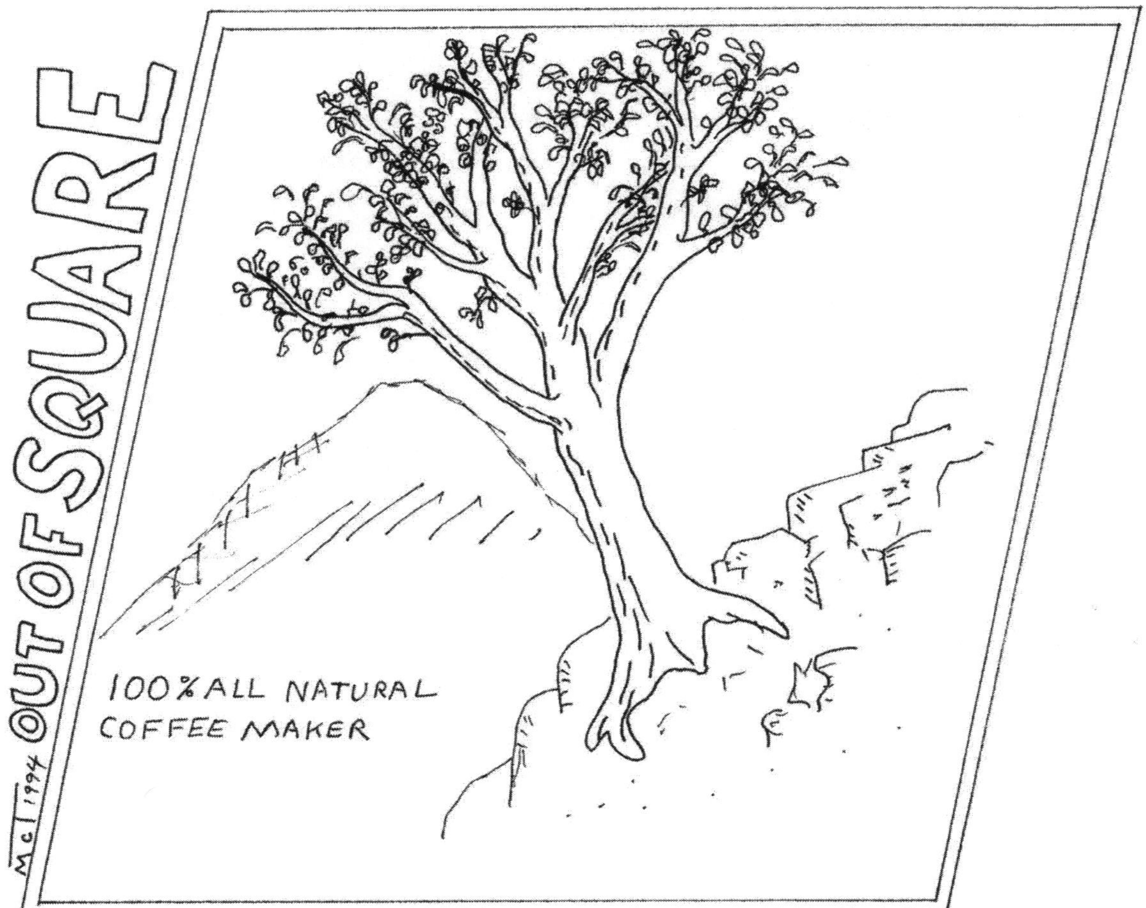
OUT OF SQUARE
McT 1994
100% ALL NATURAL
COFFEE MAKER

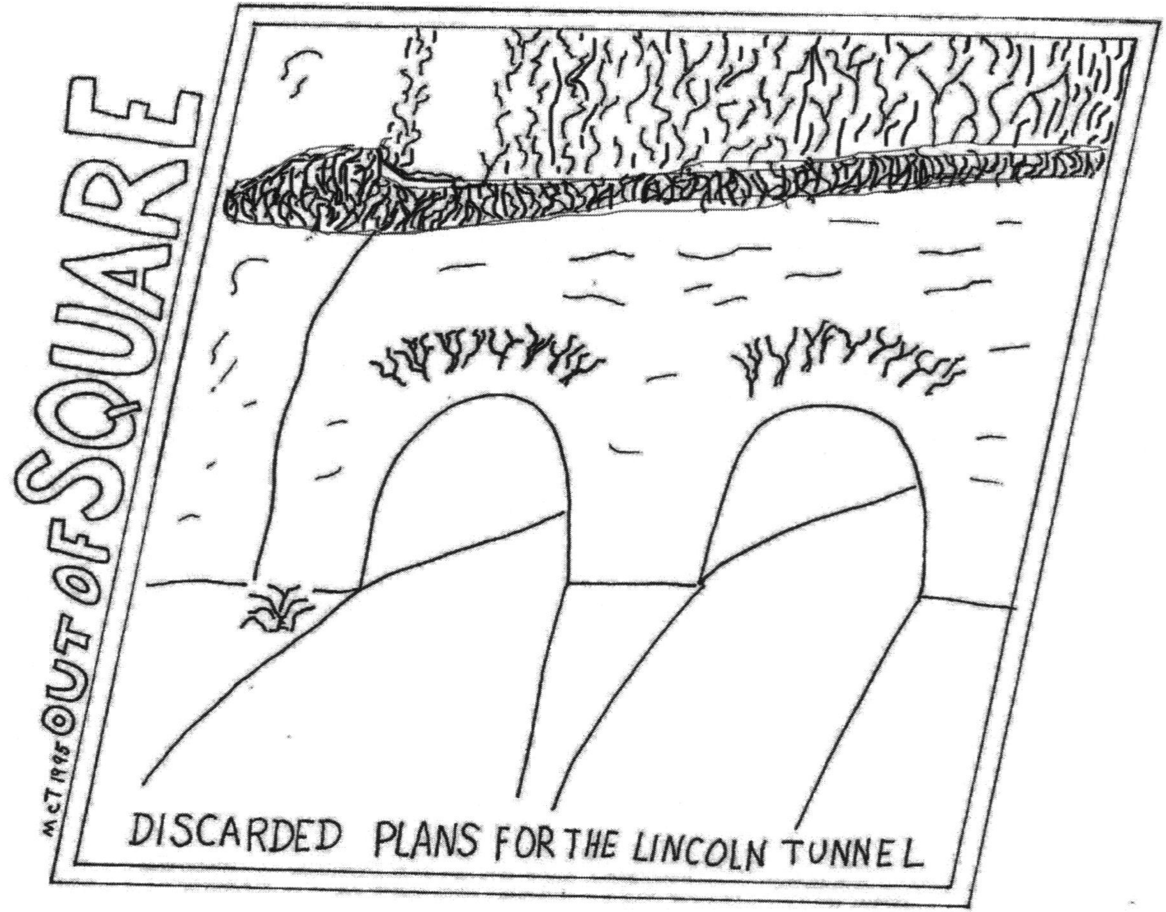
OUT OF SQUARE
McT 1995
DISCARDED PLANS FOR THE LINCOLN TUNNEL

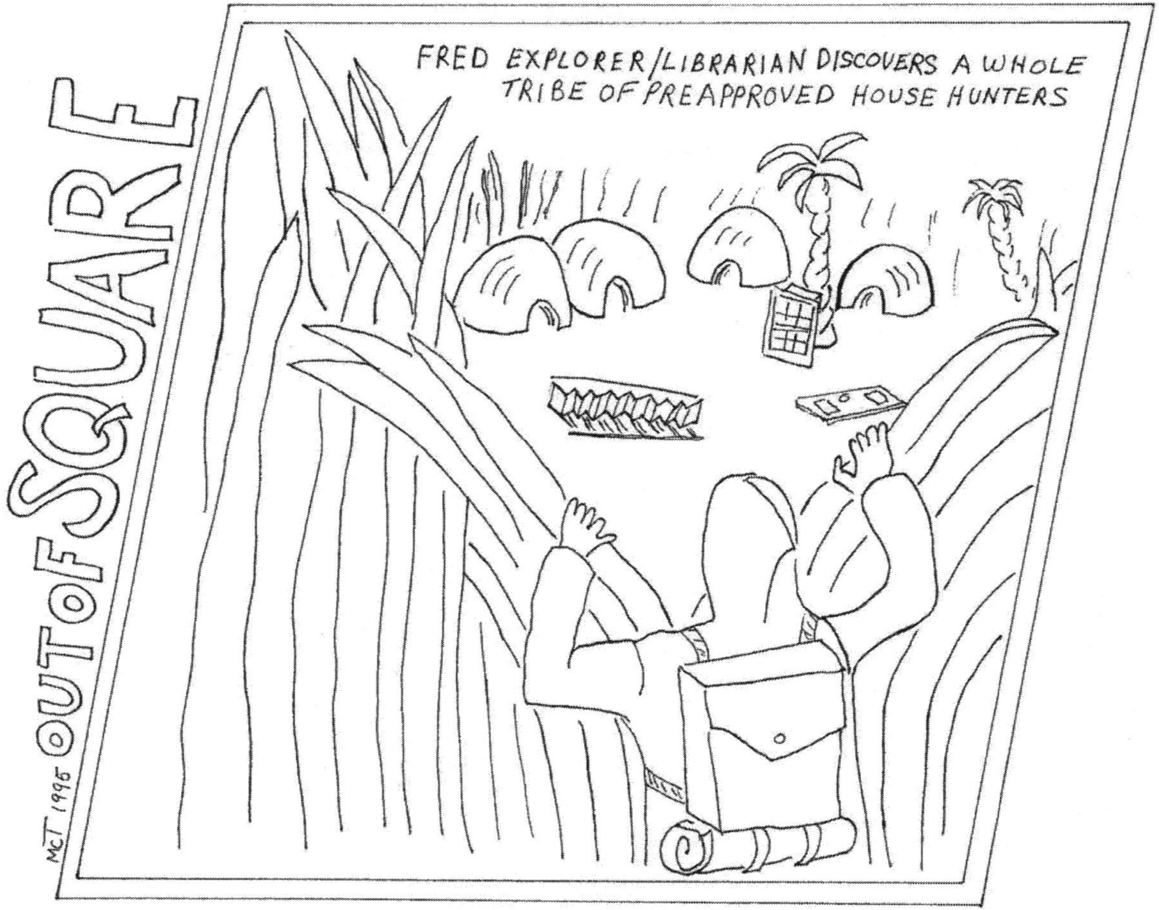
OUT of SQUARE
MCT 1995
FRED EXPLORER/LIBRARIAN DISCOVERS A WHOLE
TRIBE OF PREAPPROVED HOUSE HUNTERS

OUT OF SQUARE

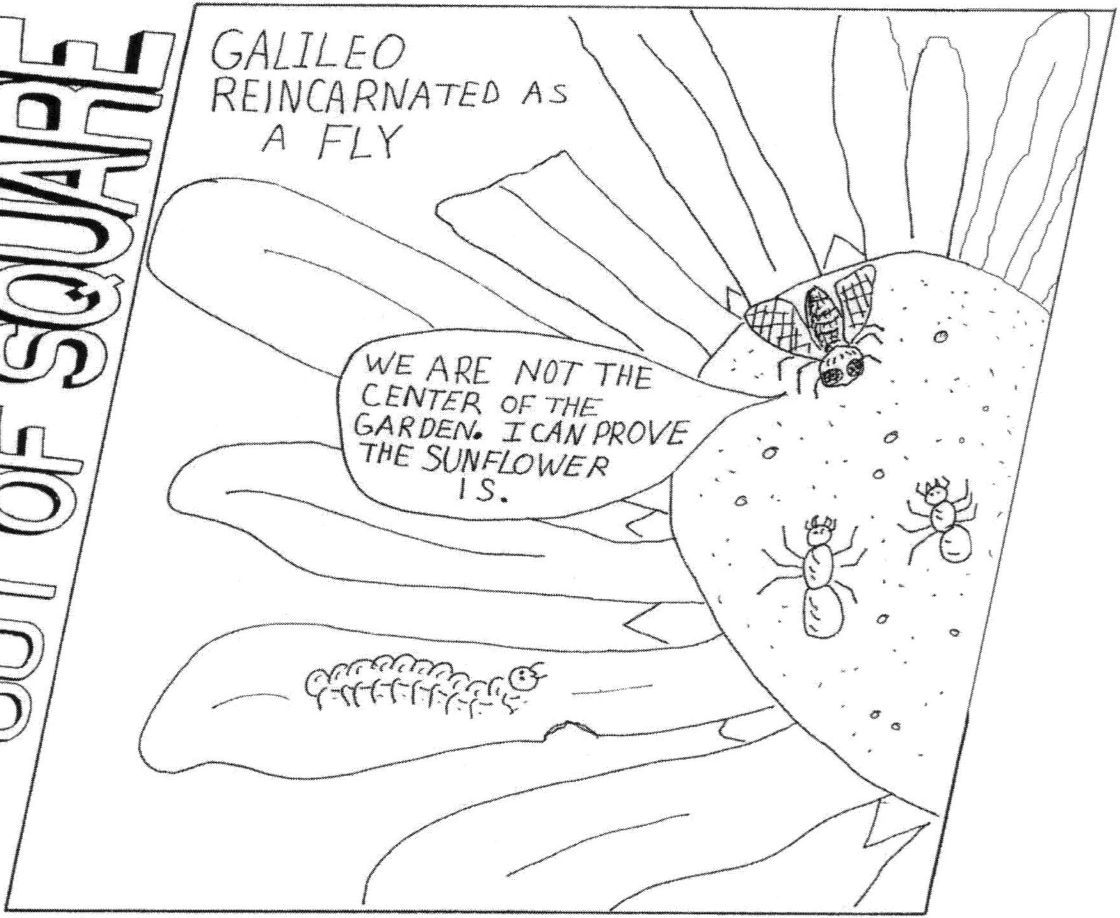
GALILEO REINCARNATED AS A FLY
WE ARE NOT THE CENTER OF THE GARDEN. I CAN PROVE THE SUNFLOWER IS.

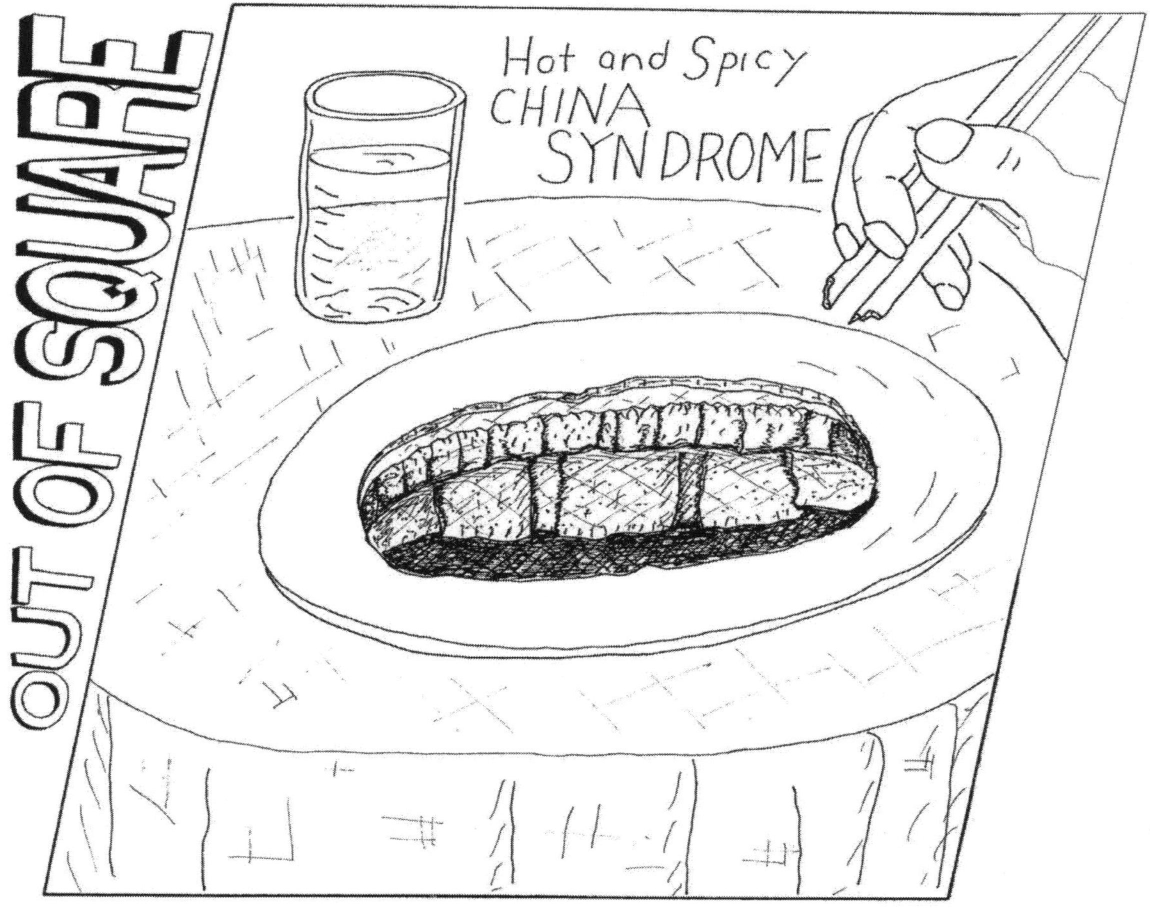
OUT OF SQUARE
Hot and Spicy
CHINA
SYNDROME

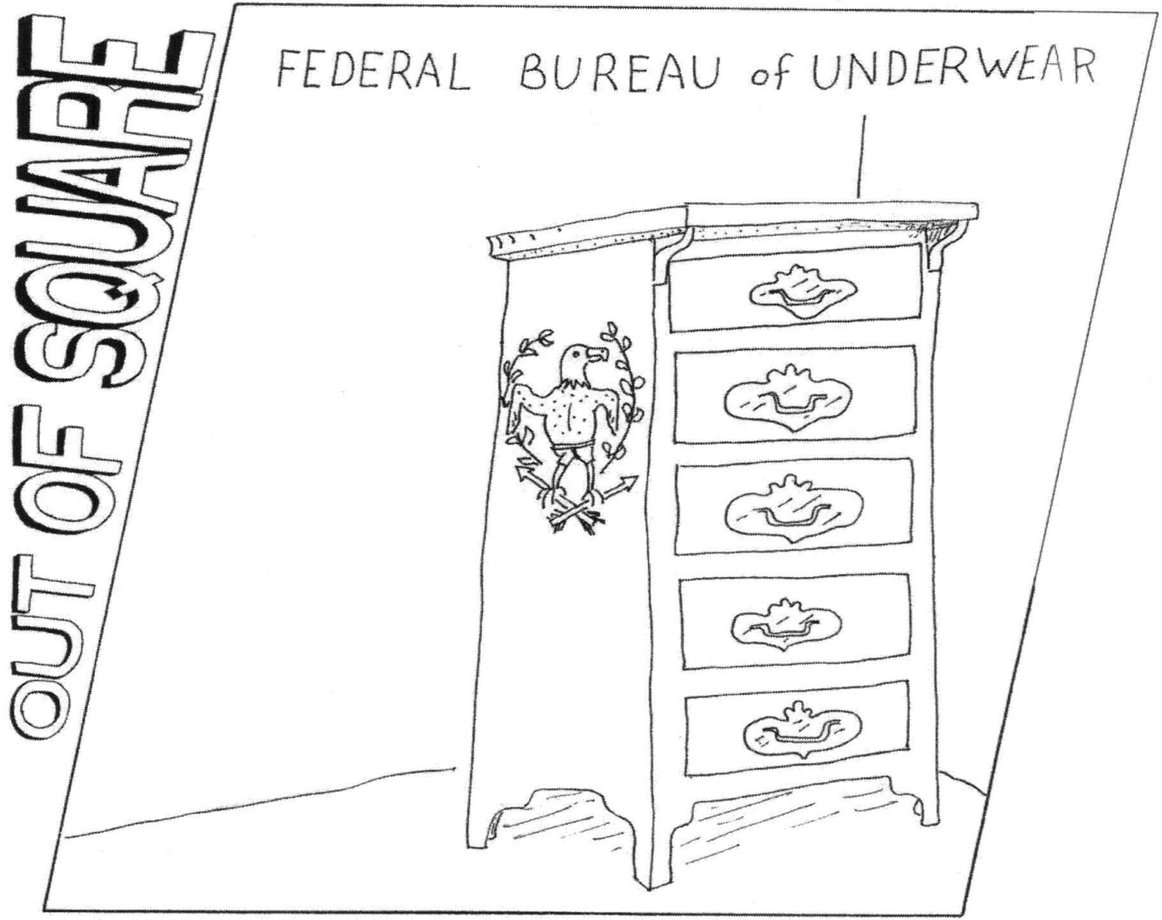
OUT OF SQUARE
FEDERAL BUREAU of UNDERWEAR

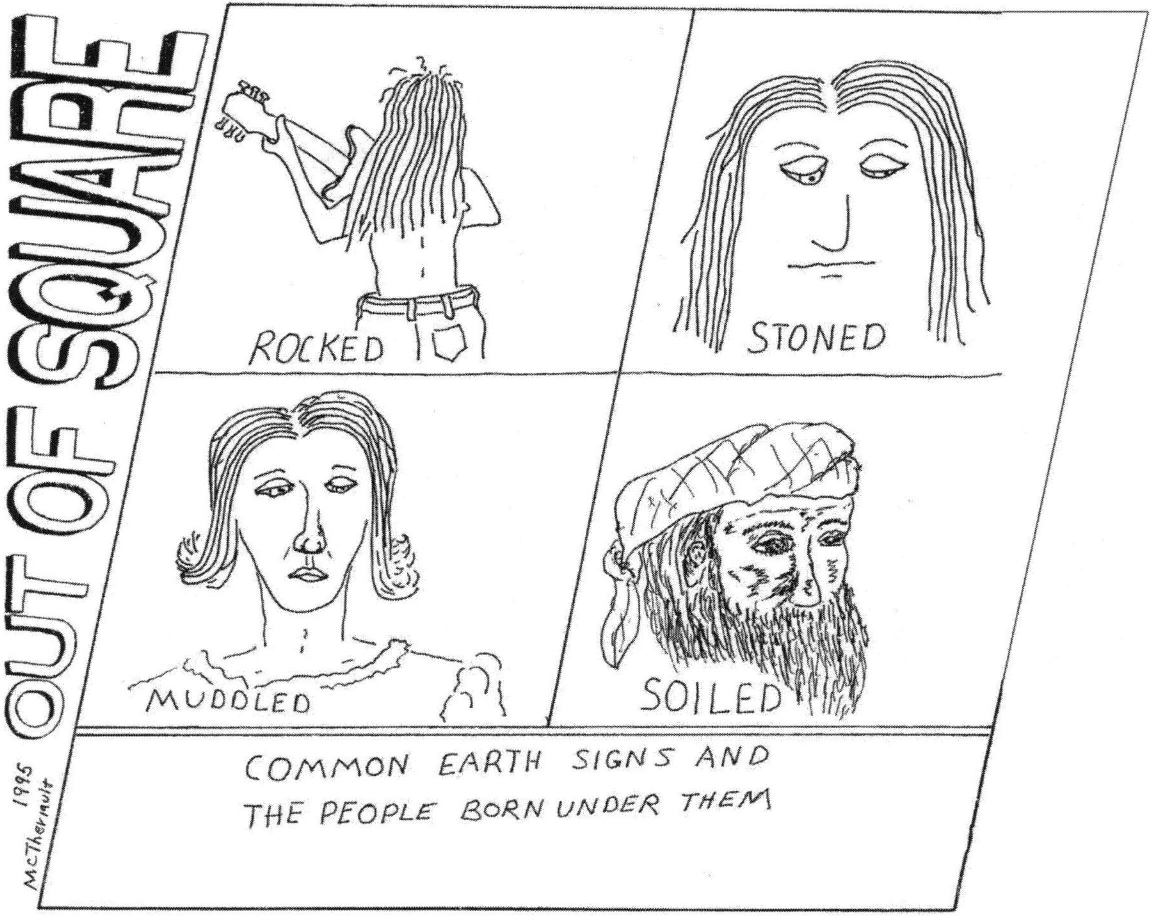
OUT OF SQUARE
ROCKED
STONED
MUDDLED
SOILED
COMMON EARTH SIGNS AND
THE PEOPLE BORN UNDER THEM
1995
McTheriault

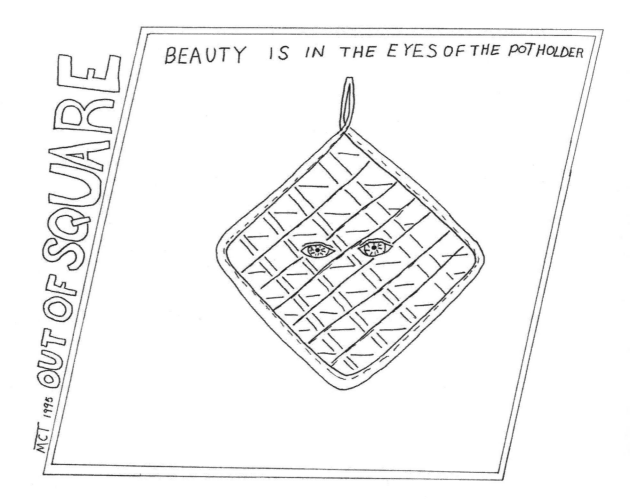

BEAUTY IS IN THE EYES OF THE POTHOLDER

OUT OF SQUARE

MCT 1995

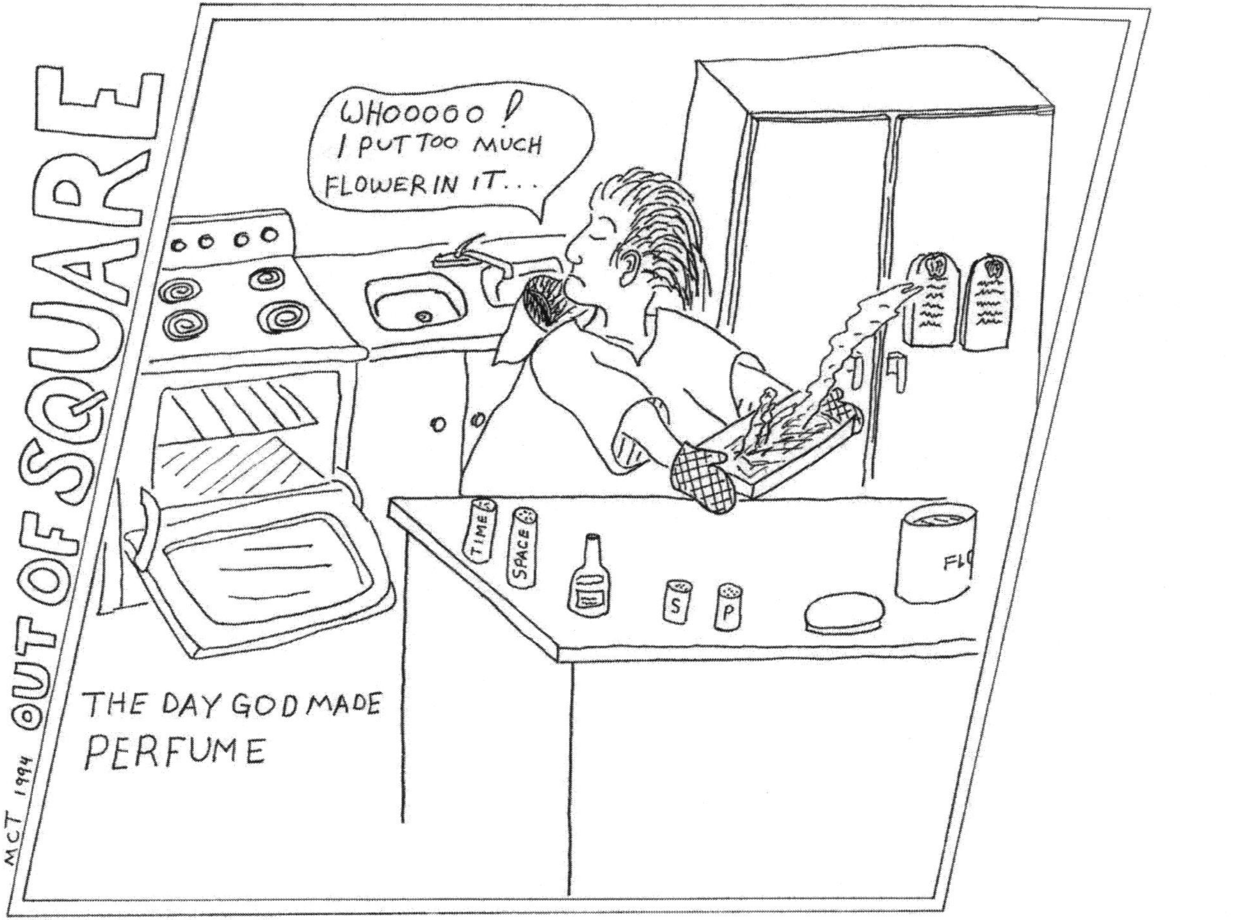

OUT OF SQUARE
WHOOOOO! I PUT TOO MUCH FLOWER IN IT...
TIME
SPACE
S
P
THE DAY GOD MADE PERFUME
MCT 1994

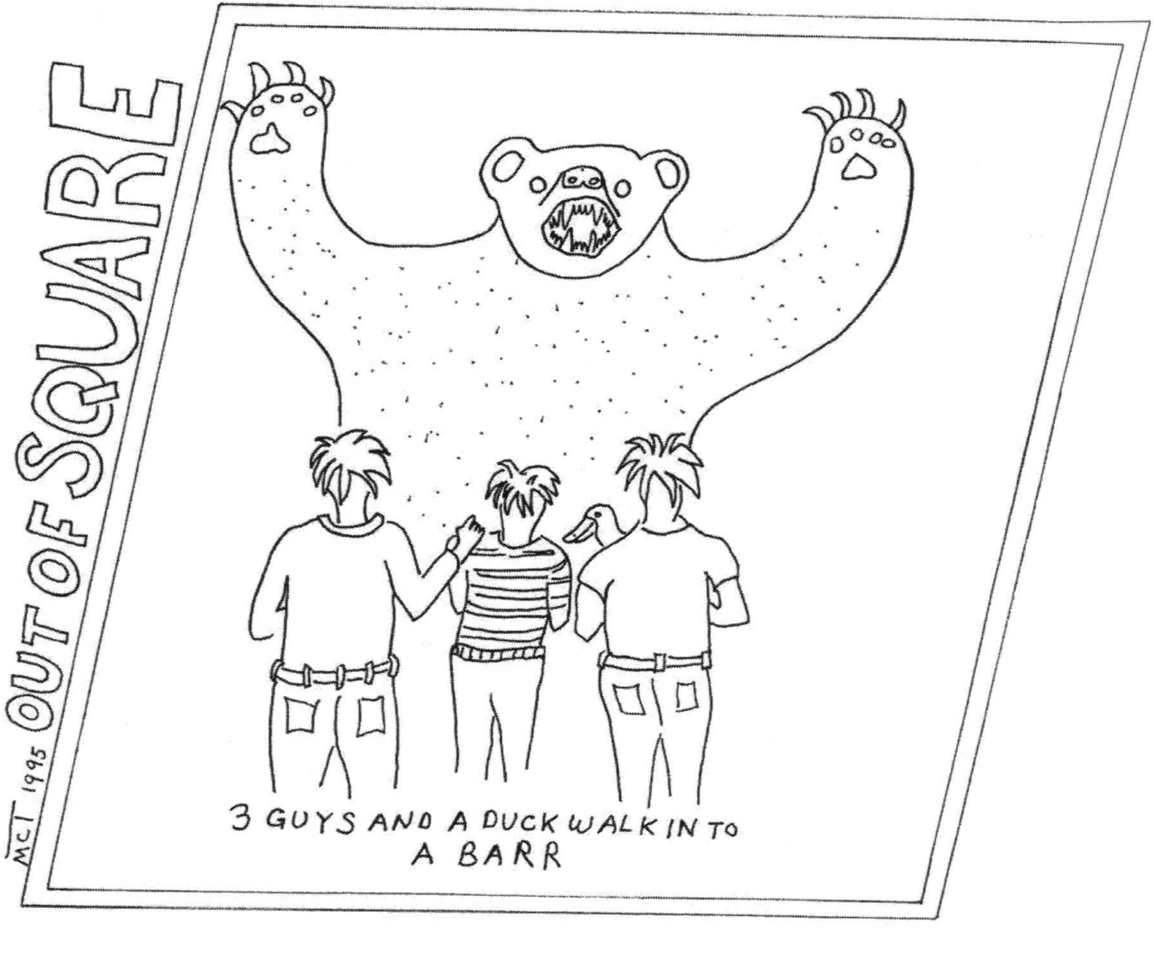
OUT OF SQUARE
MCT 1995

3 GUYS AND A DUCK WALK IN TO A BARR

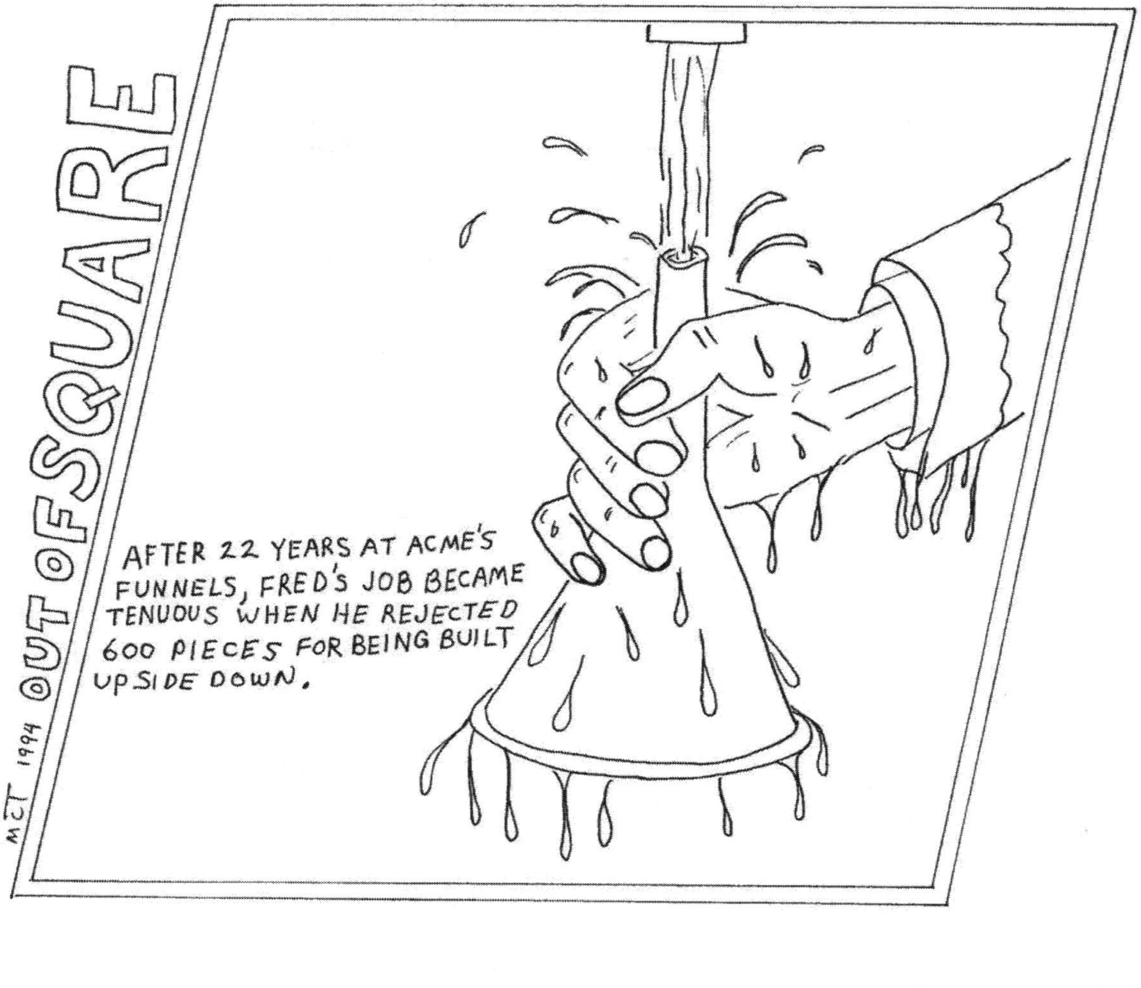
OUT OF SQUARE
MCT 1994
AFTER 22 YEARS AT ACME'S FUNNELS, FRED'S JOB BECAME TENUOUS WHEN HE REJECTED 600 PIECES FOR BEING BUILT UPSIDE DOWN.

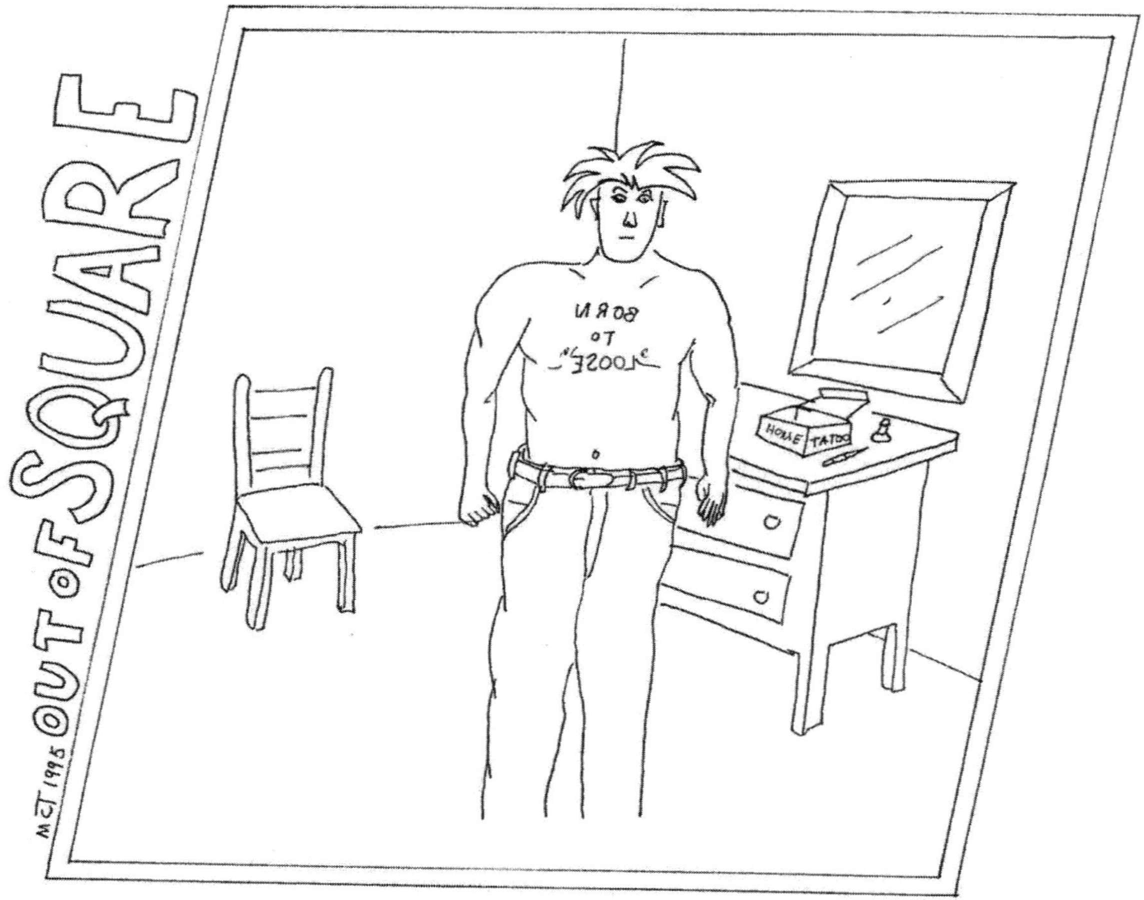
OUT OF SQUARE
MCT 1995
BORN TO "LOOSE"
HOME TATOO

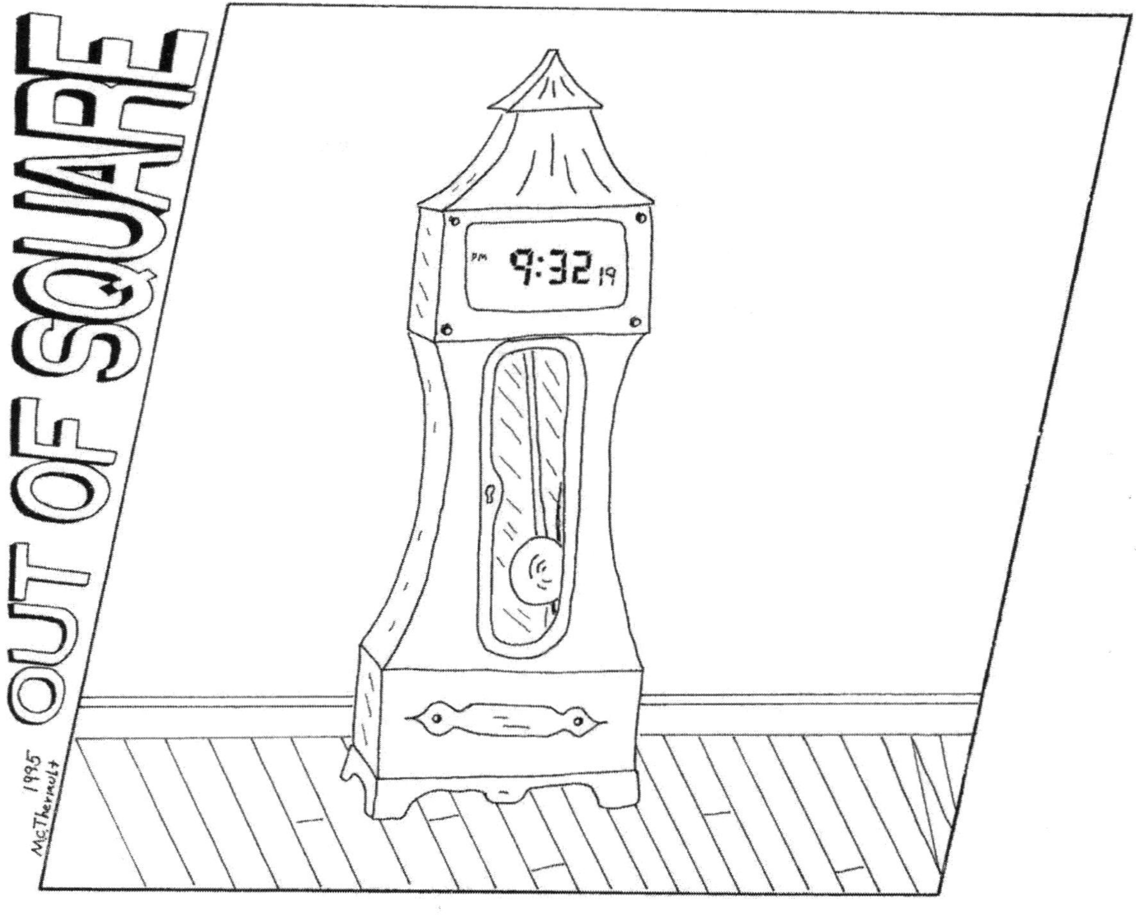
OUT OF SQUARE
PM
9:32 19
1995
McTheriault

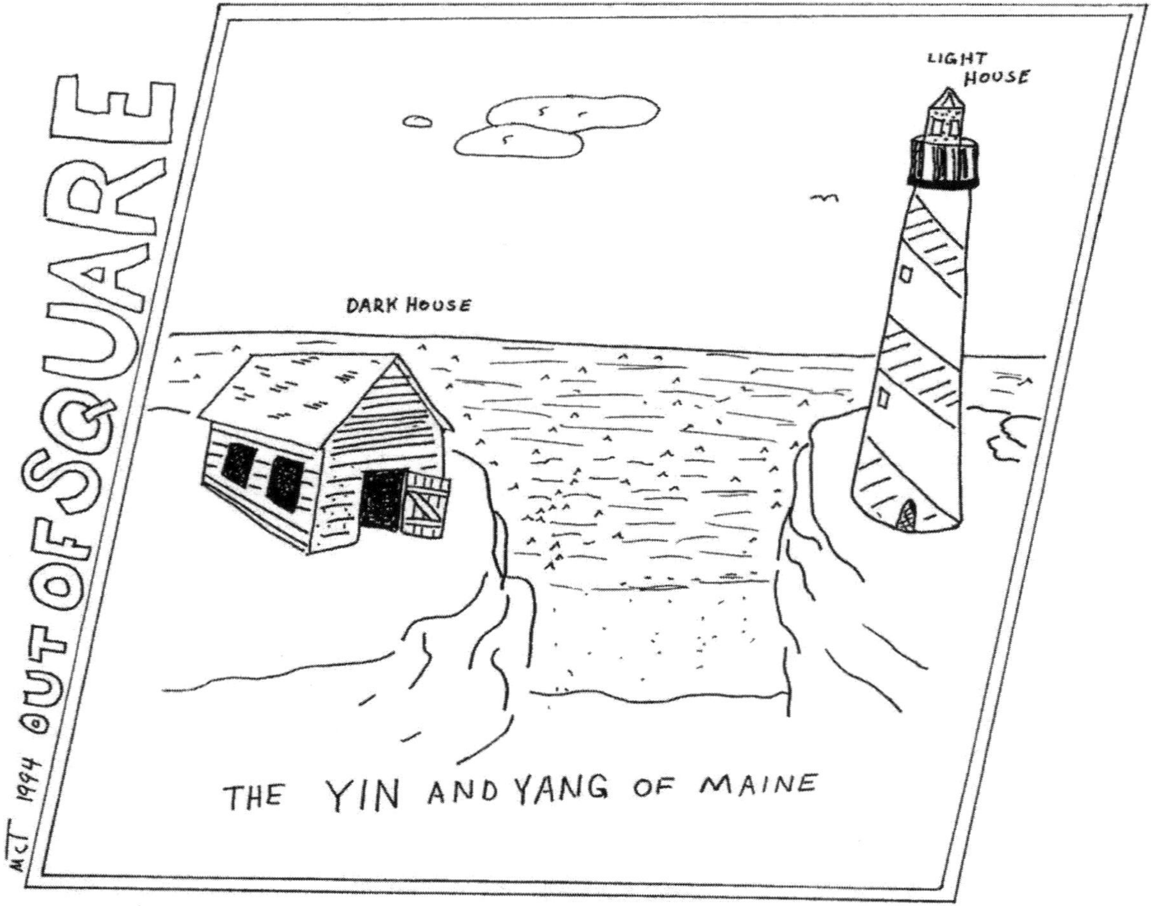
OUT OF SQUARE
©1994 McT
LIGHT HOUSE
DARK HOUSE
THE YIN AND YANG OF MAINE

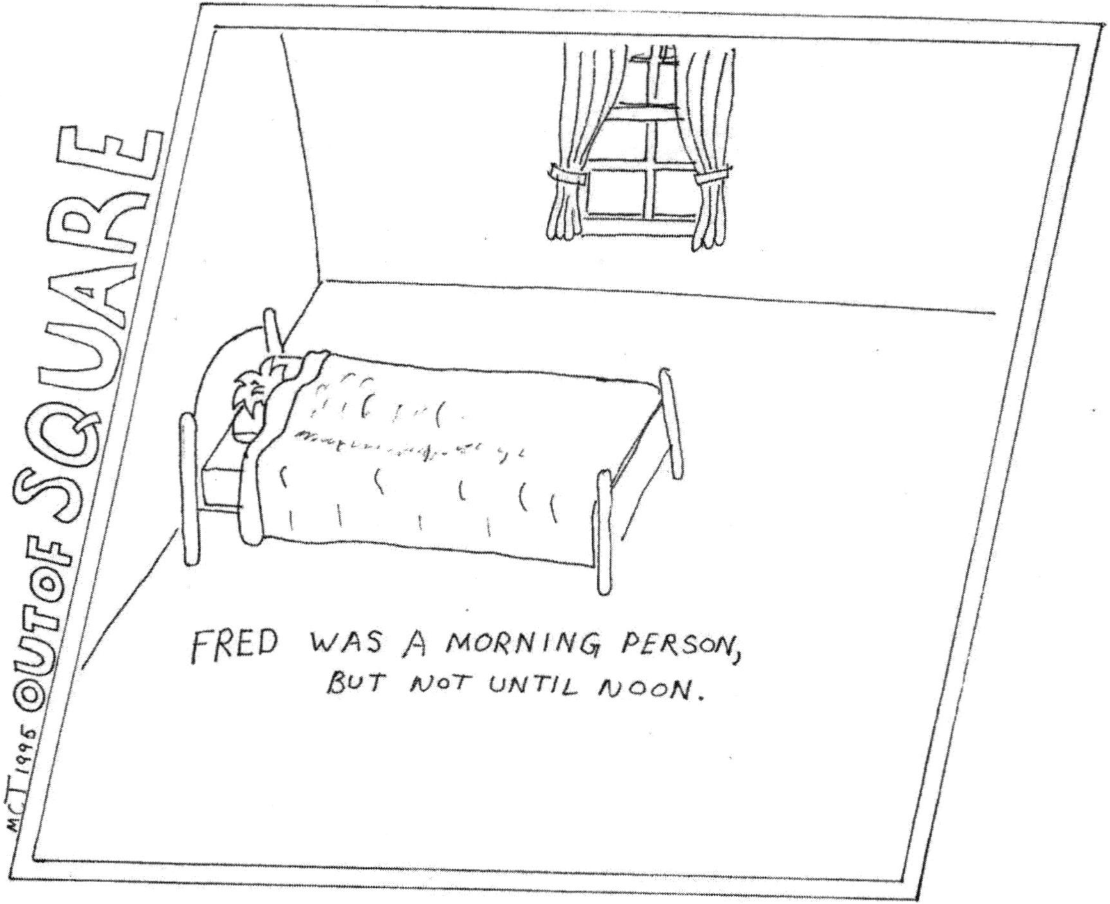
OUT OF SQUARE
MCT 1995
FRED WAS A MORNING PERSON,
BUT NOT UNTIL NOON.

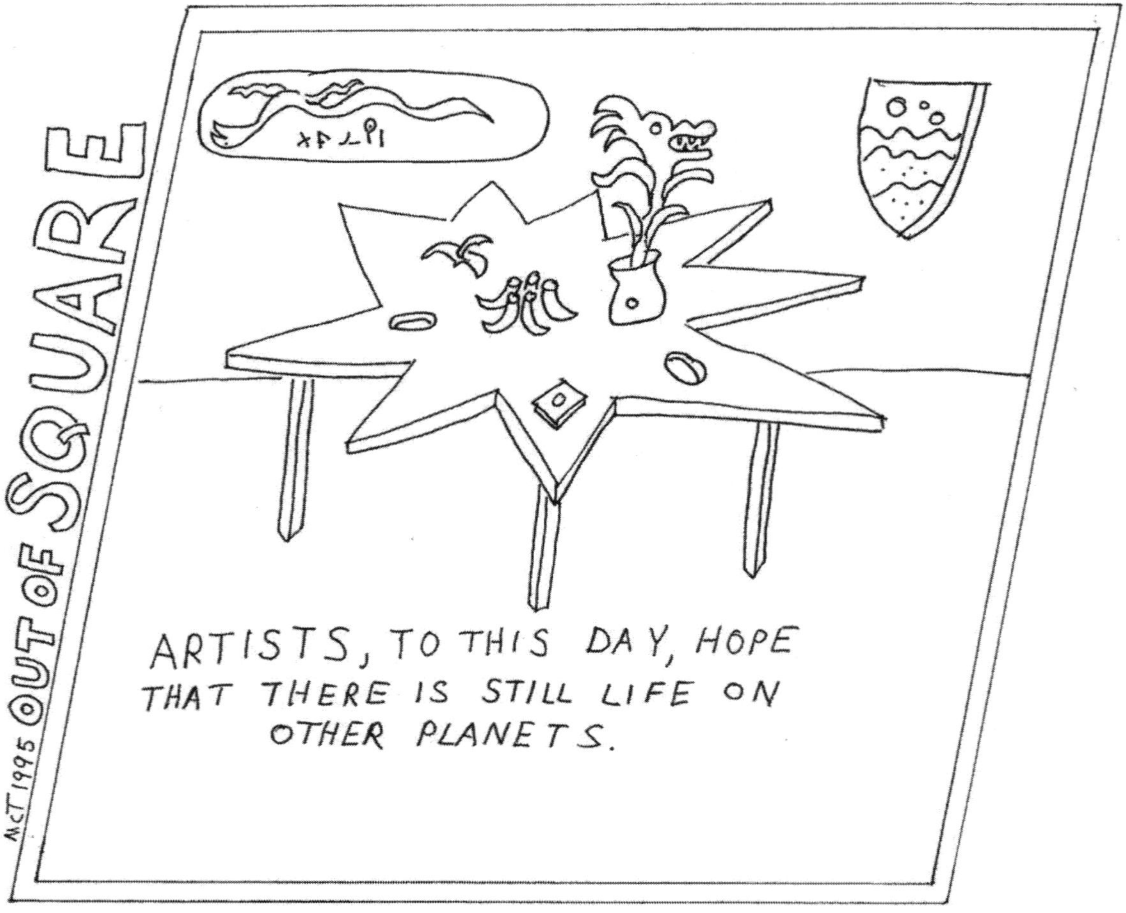
OUT OF SQUARE
McT 1995
ARTISTS, TO THIS DAY, HOPE THAT THERE IS STILL LIFE ON OTHER PLANETS.

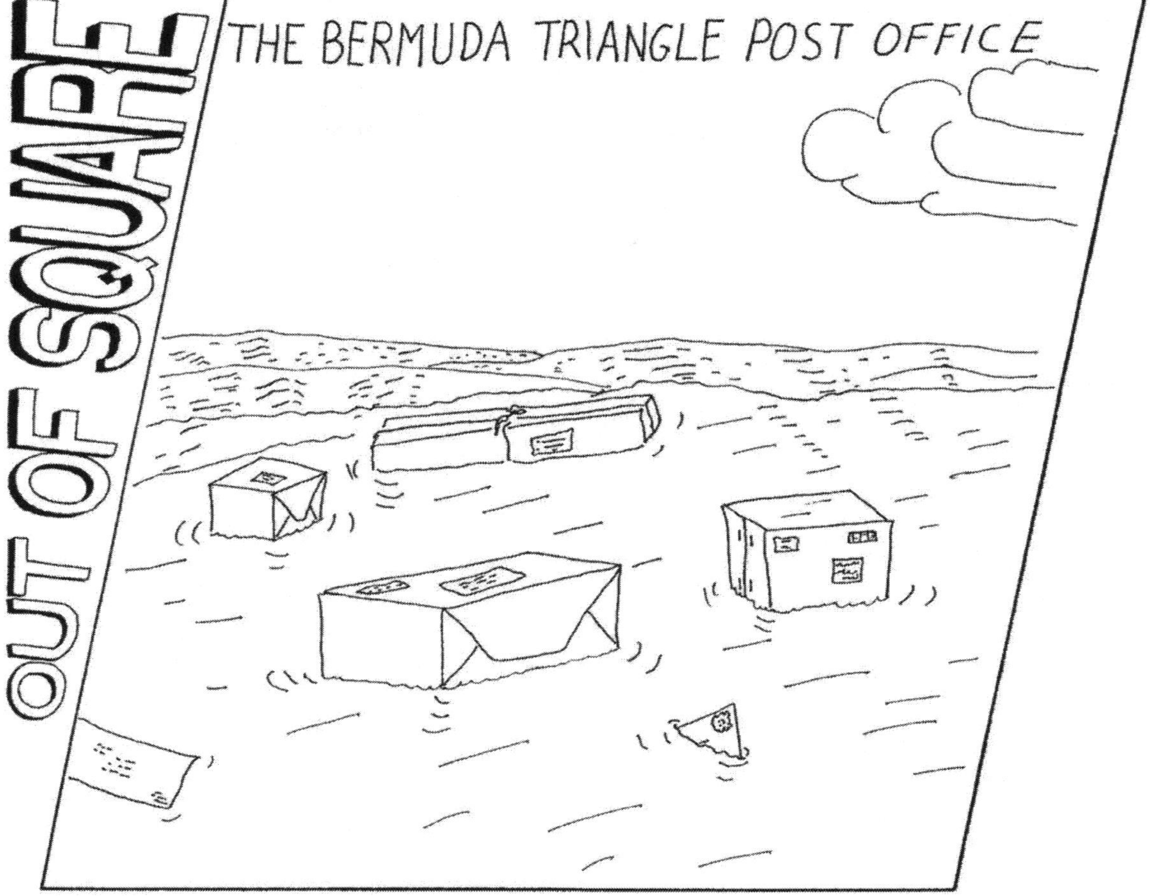
OUT OF SQUARE
THE BERMUDA TRIANGLE POST OFFICE

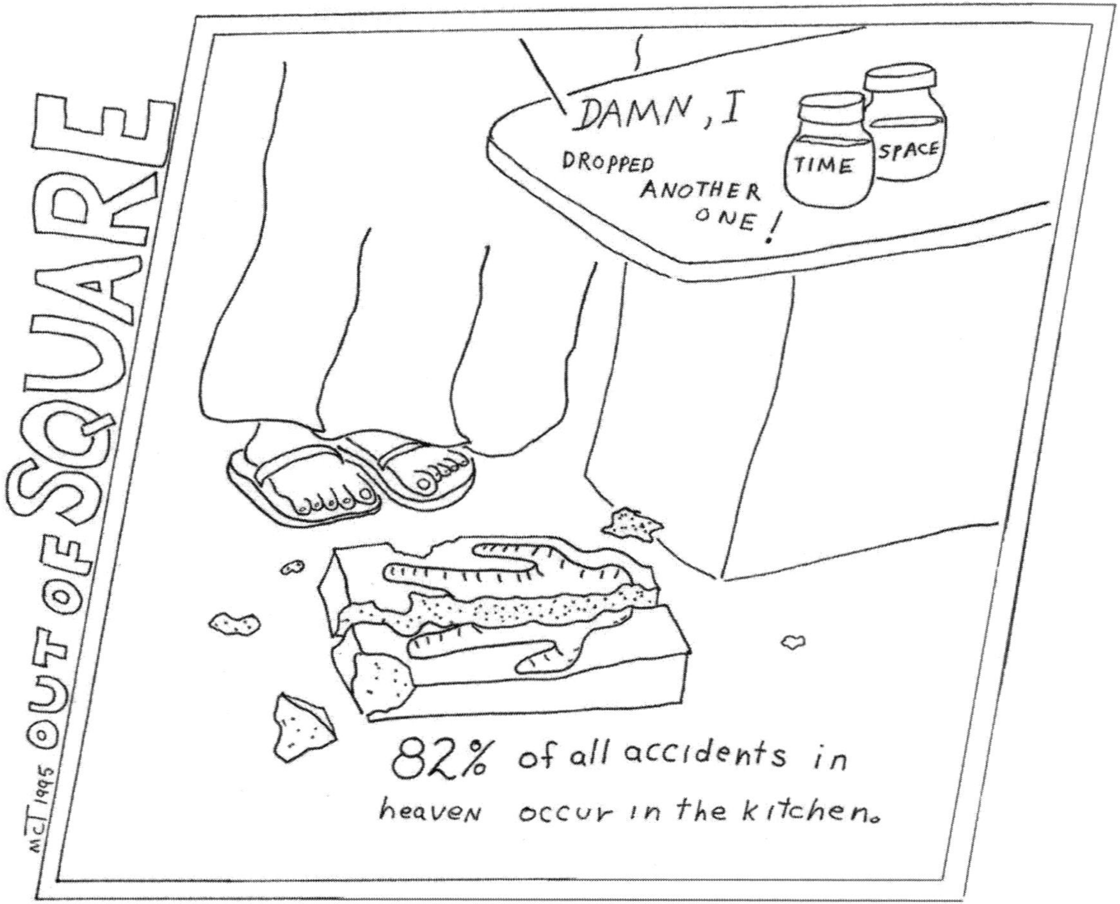
OUT OF SQUARE
McT 1995
DAMN, I DROPPED ANOTHER ONE!
TIME
SPACE
82% of all accidents in heaven occur in the kitchen.

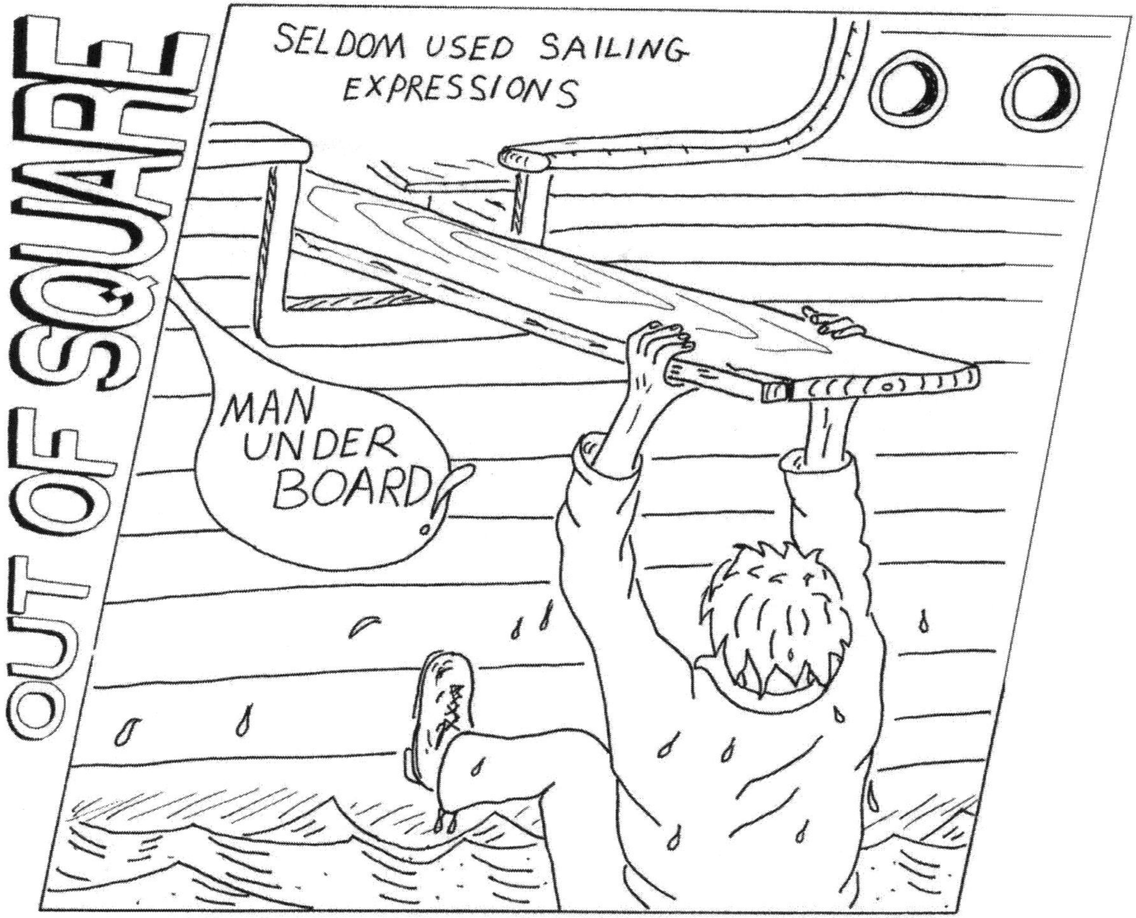
OUT OF SQUARE
SELDOM USED SAILING EXPRESSIONS
MAN UNDER BOARD!

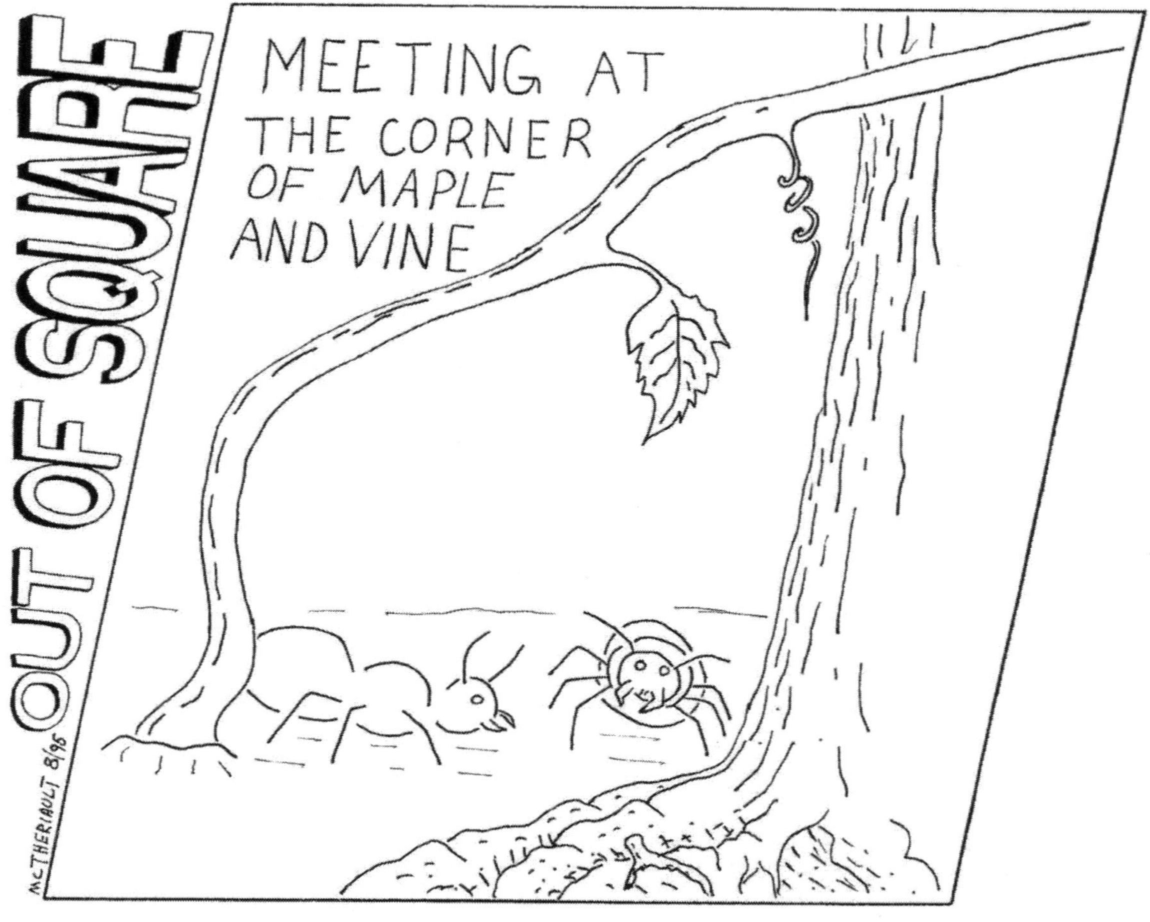
OUT OF SQUARE
MEETING AT THE CORNER OF MAPLE AND VINE
M.C. THERIAULT 8/96

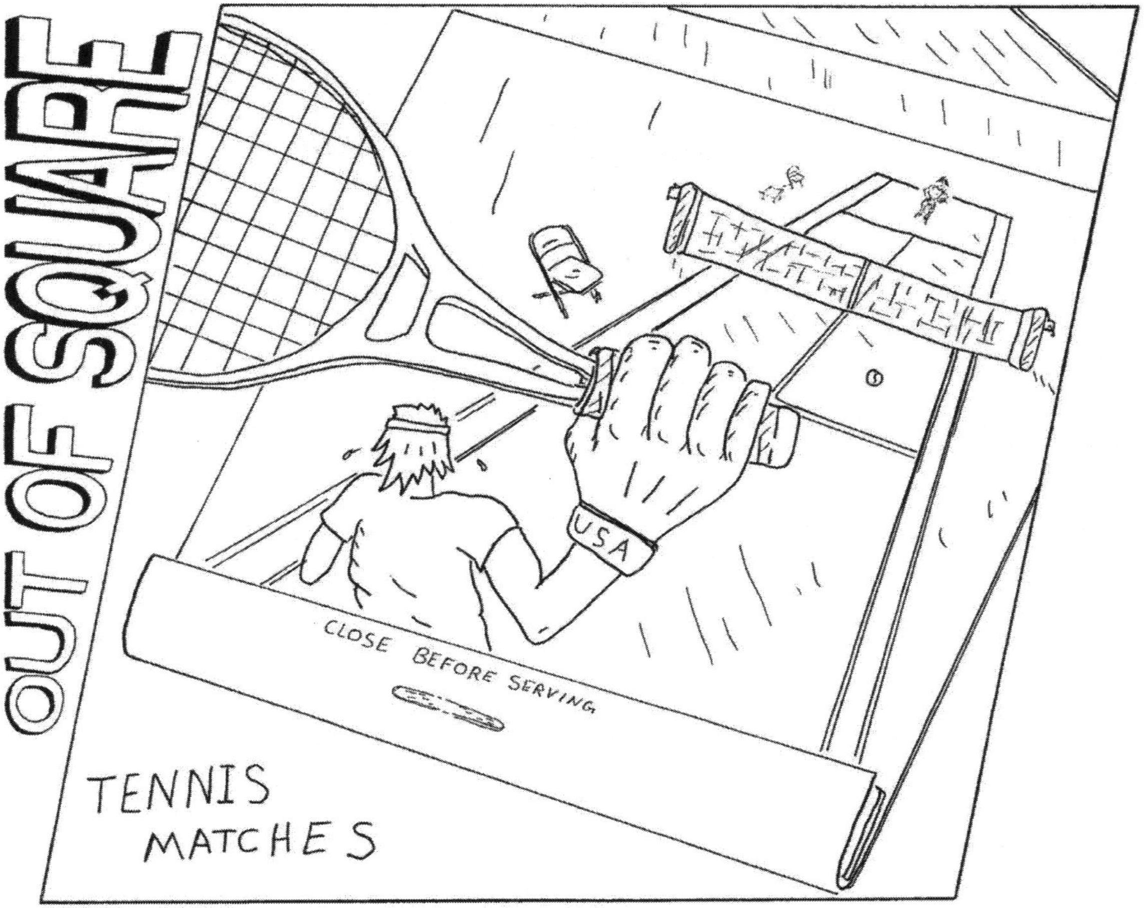
OUT OF SQUARE
USA
CLOSE BEFORE SERVING
TENNIS
MATCHES

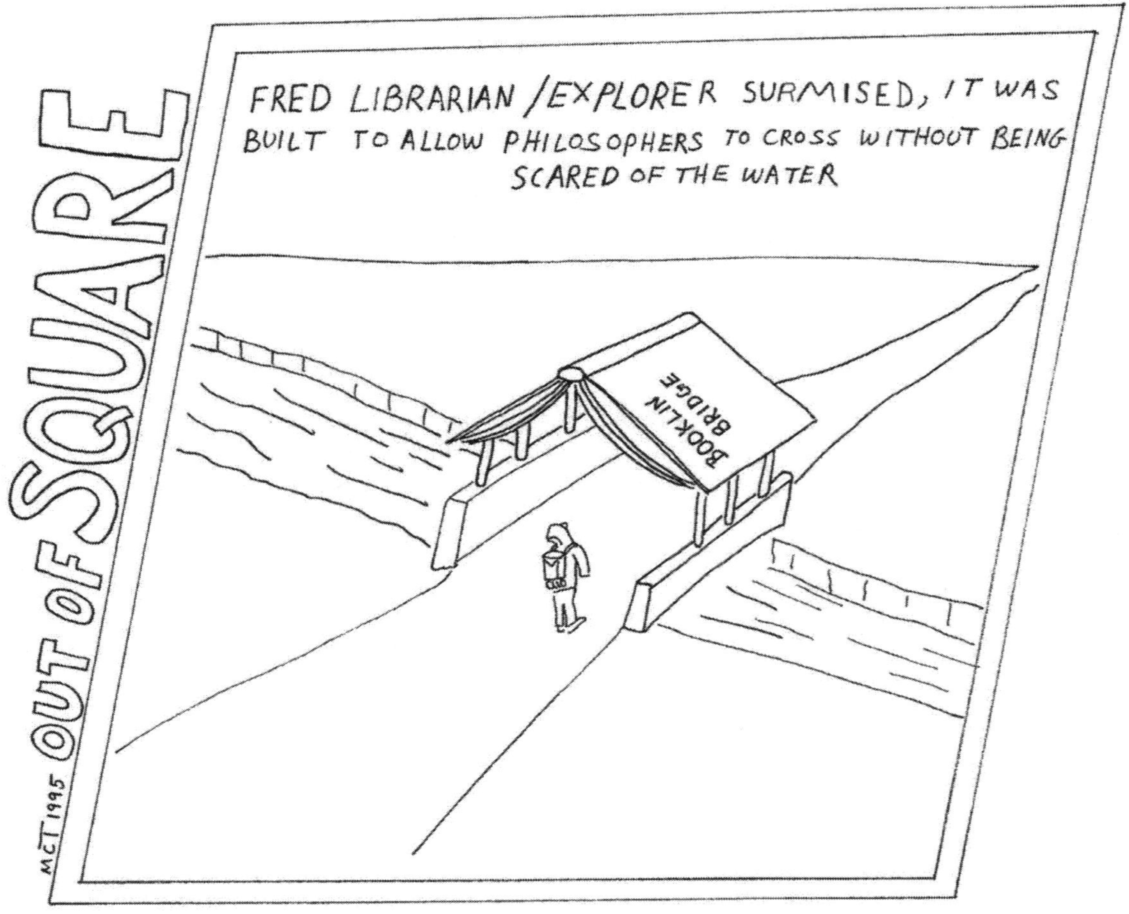
OUT OF SQUARE
MCT 1995
FRED LIBRARIAN / EXPLORER SURMISED, IT WAS BUILT TO ALLOW PHILOSOPHERS TO CROSS WITHOUT BEING SCARED OF THE WATER
BOOKLIN BRIDGE

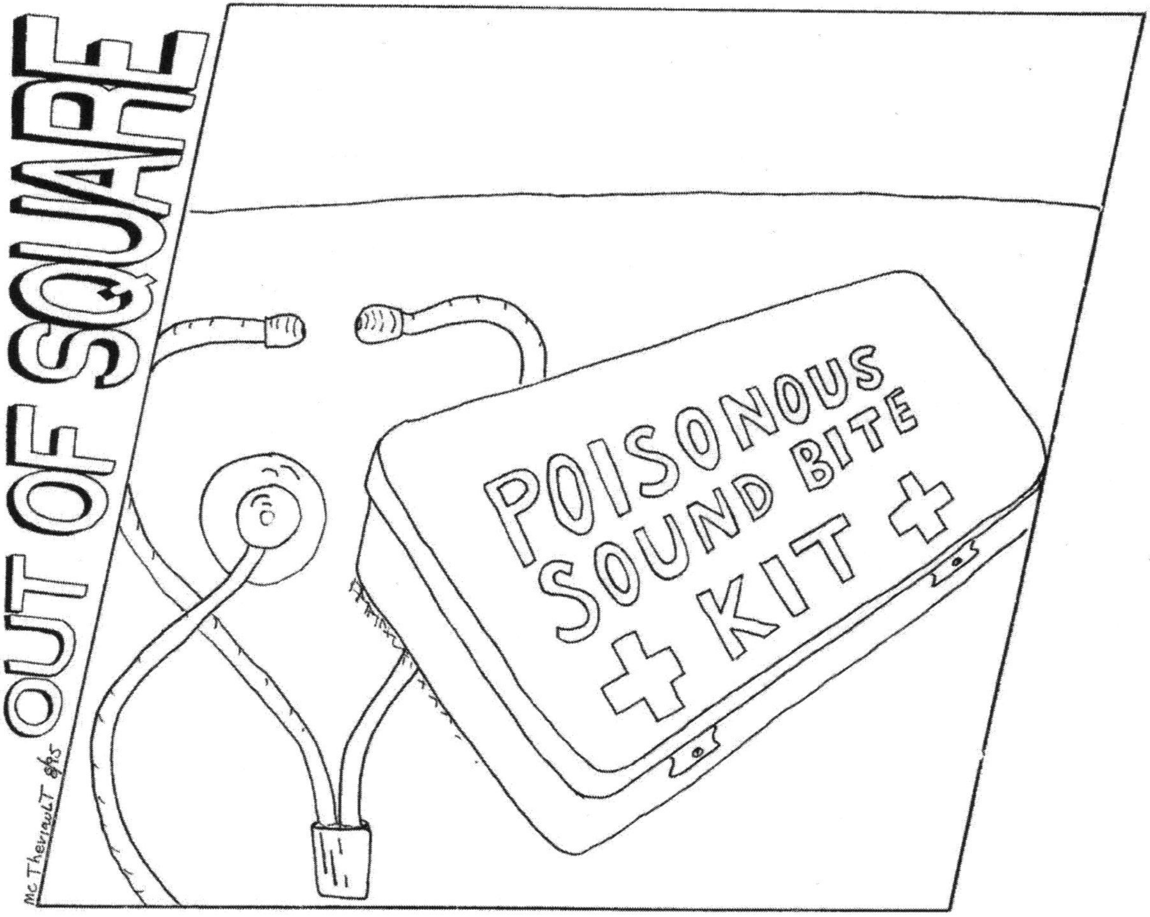
OUT OF SQUARE
POISONOUS
SOUND BITE
KIT
McTheriaulT 8/15

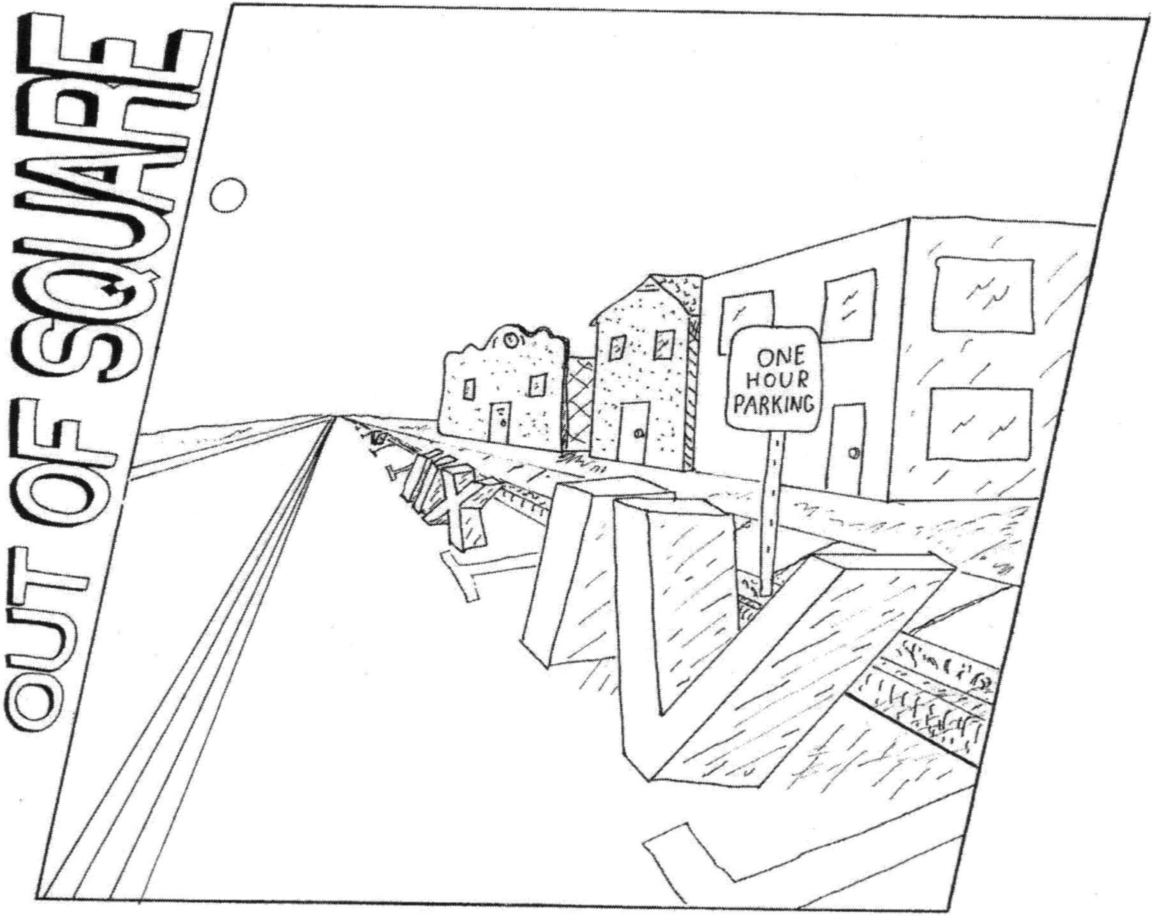
OUT OF SQUARE
ONE HOUR PARKING

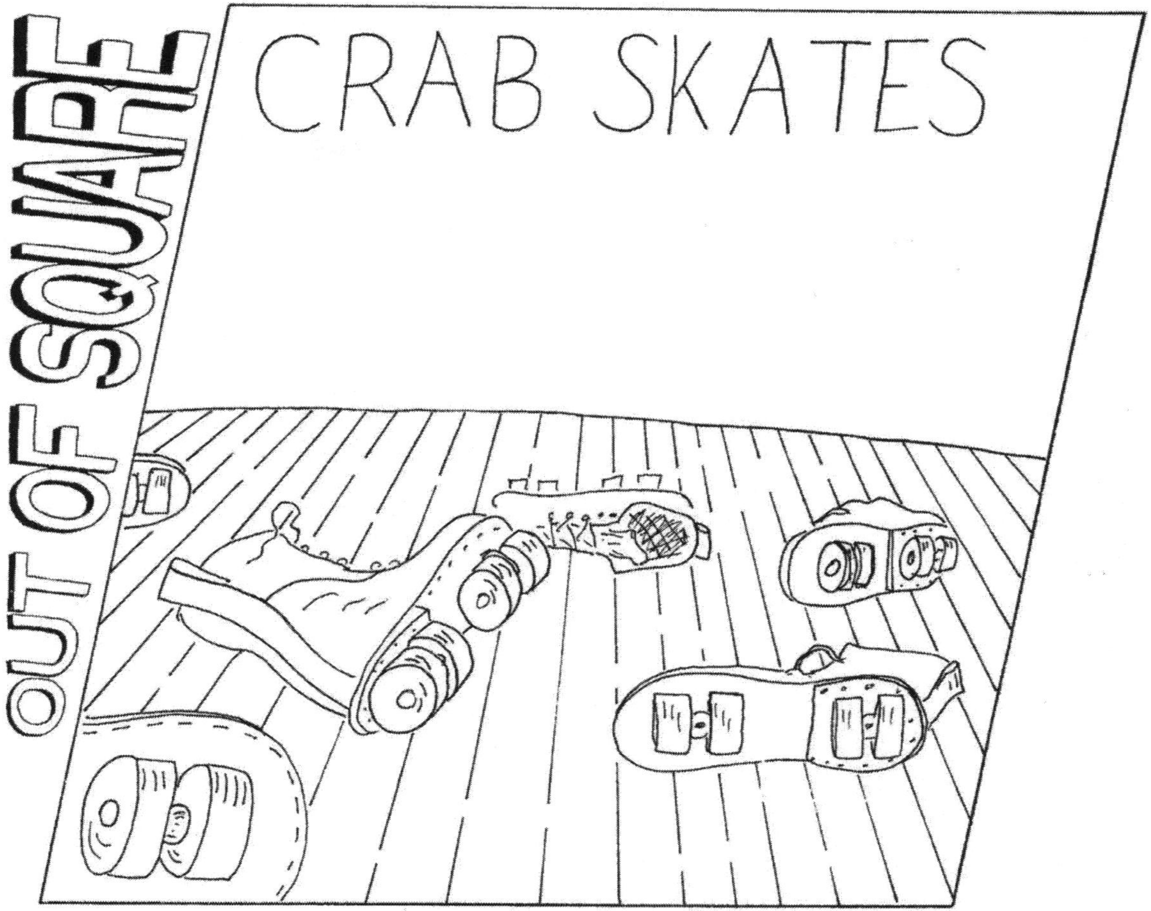
OUT OF SQUARE
CRAB SKATES

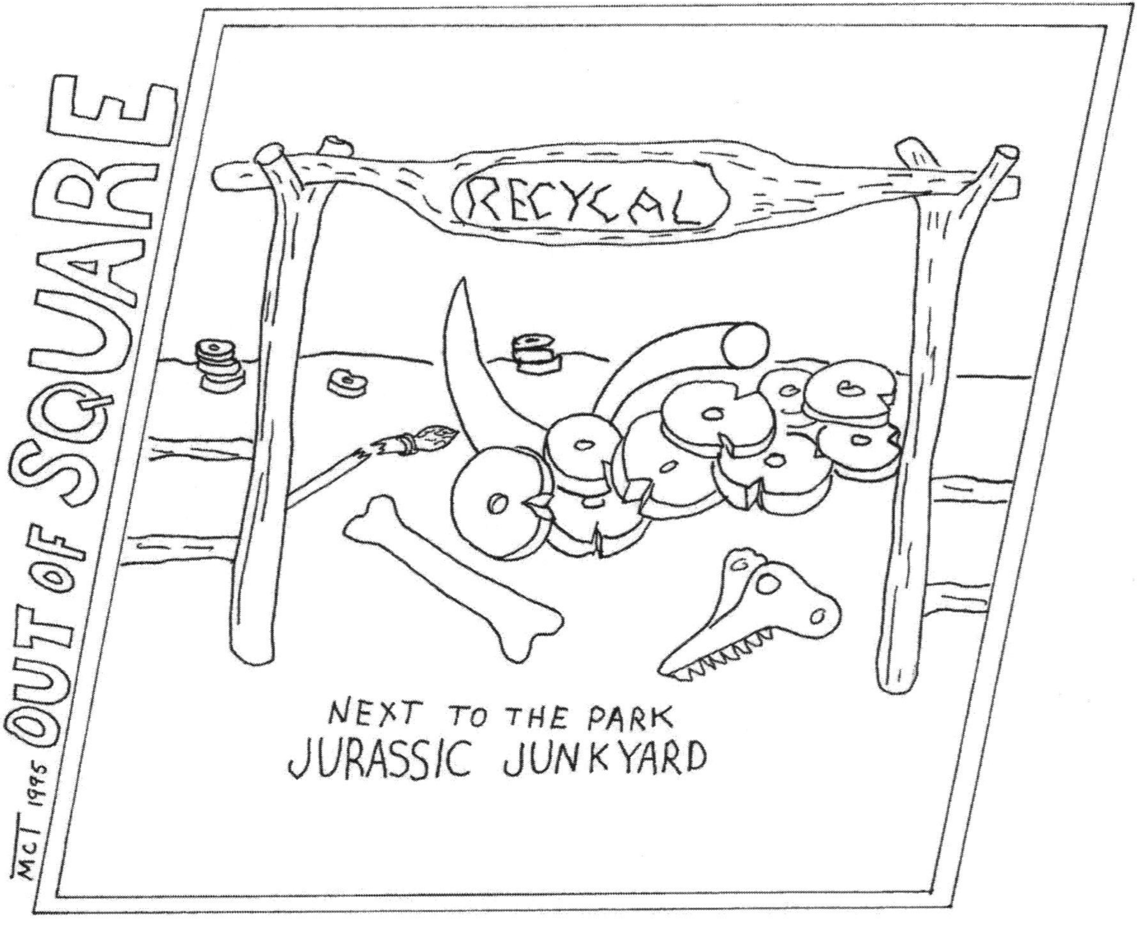
OUT OF SQUARE
MCT 1995
RECYCAL
NEXT TO THE PARK
JURASSIC JUNKYARD

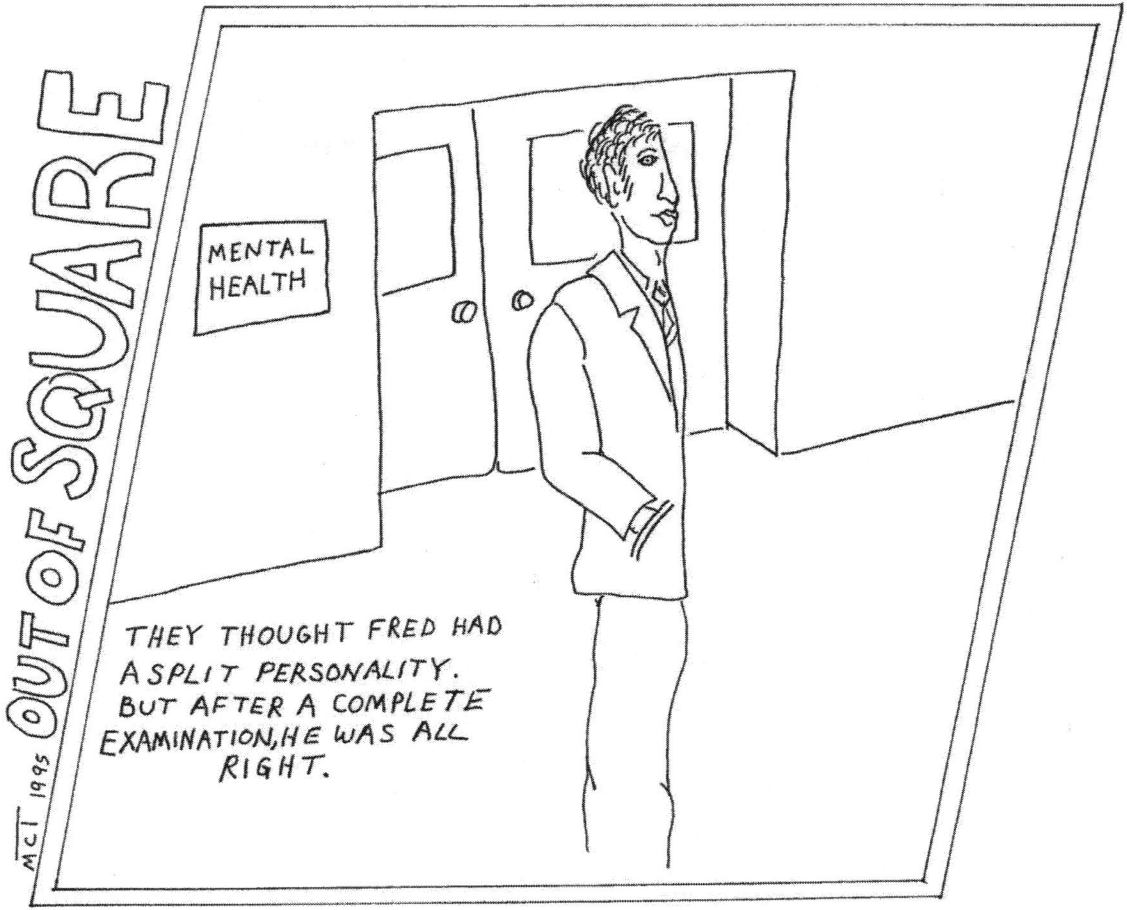
OUT OF SQUARE
MCT 1995
MENTAL HEALTH
THEY THOUGHT FRED HAD A SPLIT PERSONALITY. BUT AFTER A COMPLETE EXAMINATION, HE WAS ALL RIGHT.

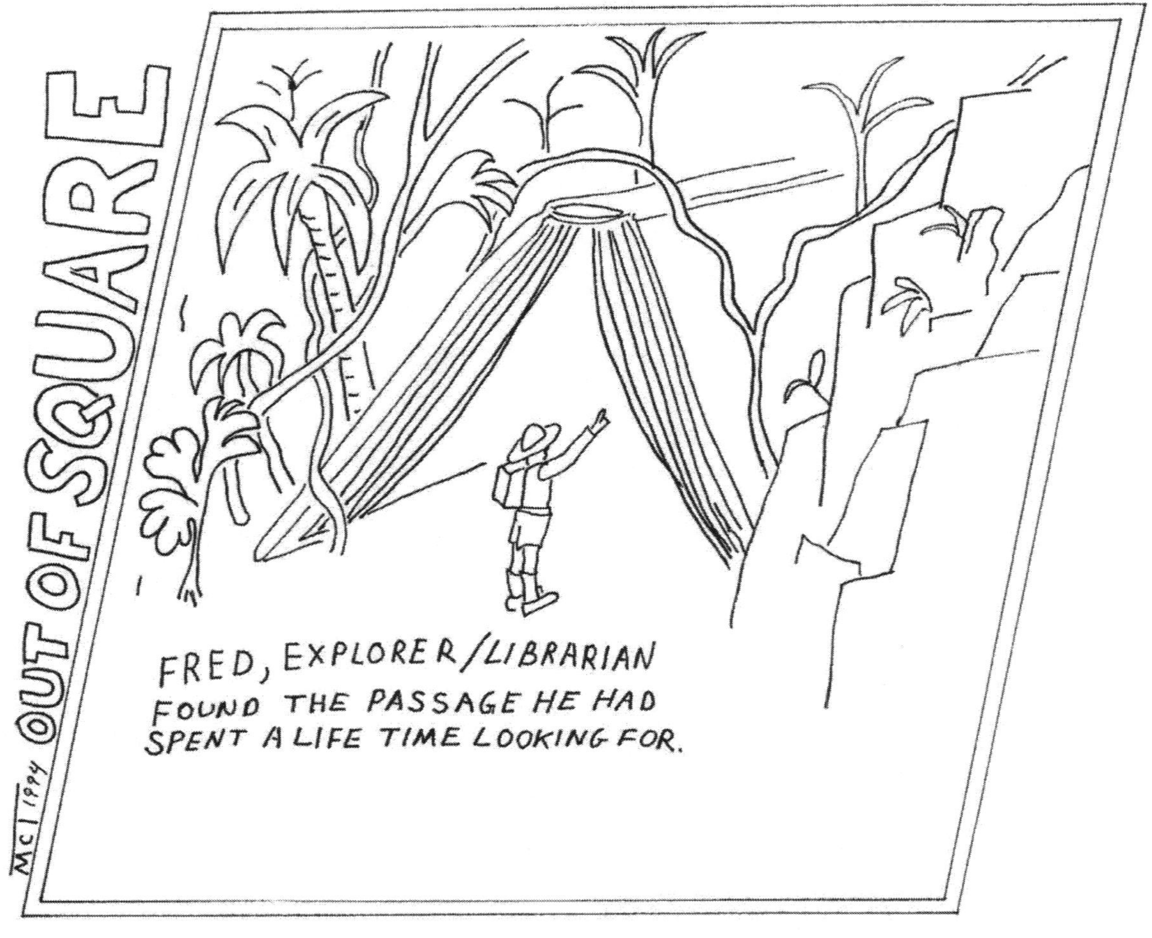
OUT OF SQUARE
MCI 1994
FRED, EXPLORER/LIBRARIAN
FOUND THE PASSAGE HE HAD
SPENT A LIFE TIME LOOKING FOR.

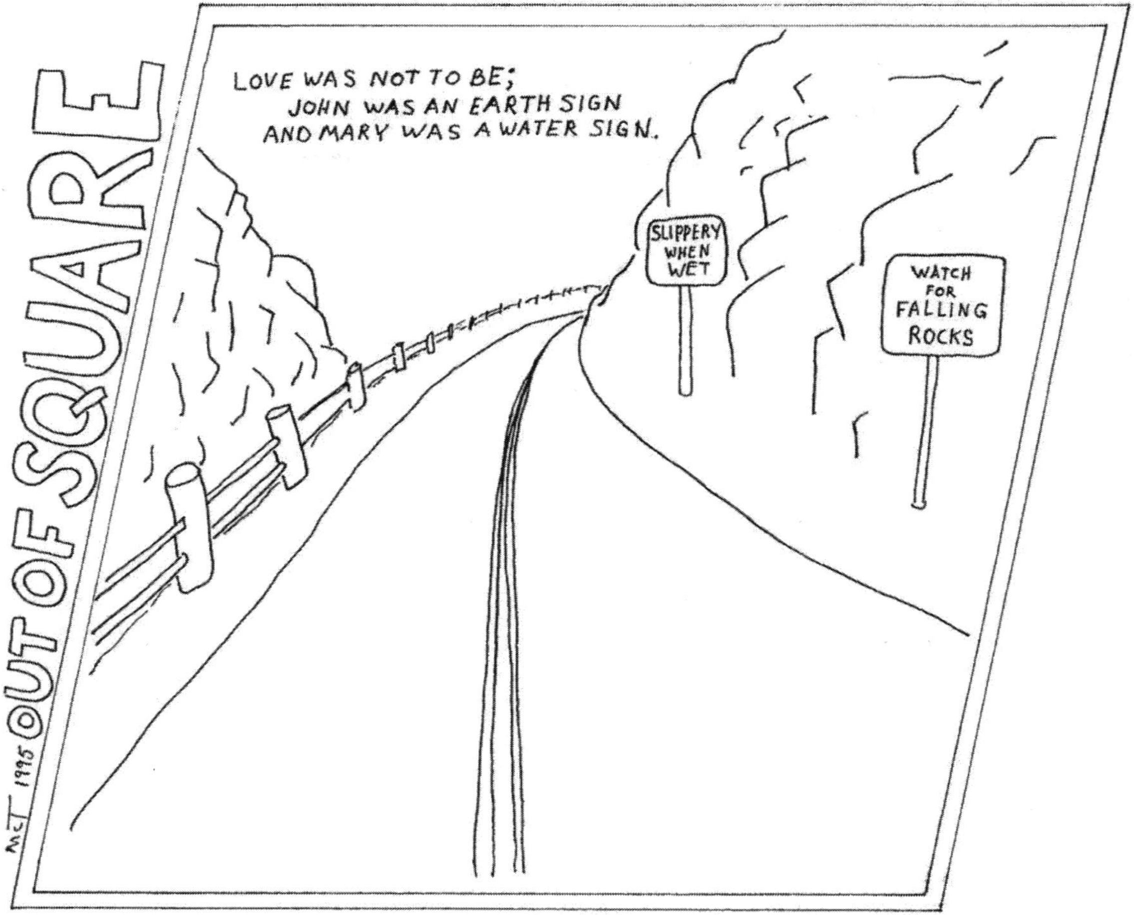
OUT OF SQUARE
MCT 1995
LOVE WAS NOT TO BE;
JOHN WAS AN EARTH SIGN
AND MARY WAS A WATER SIGN.
SLIPPERY WHEN WET
WATCH FOR FALLING ROCKS

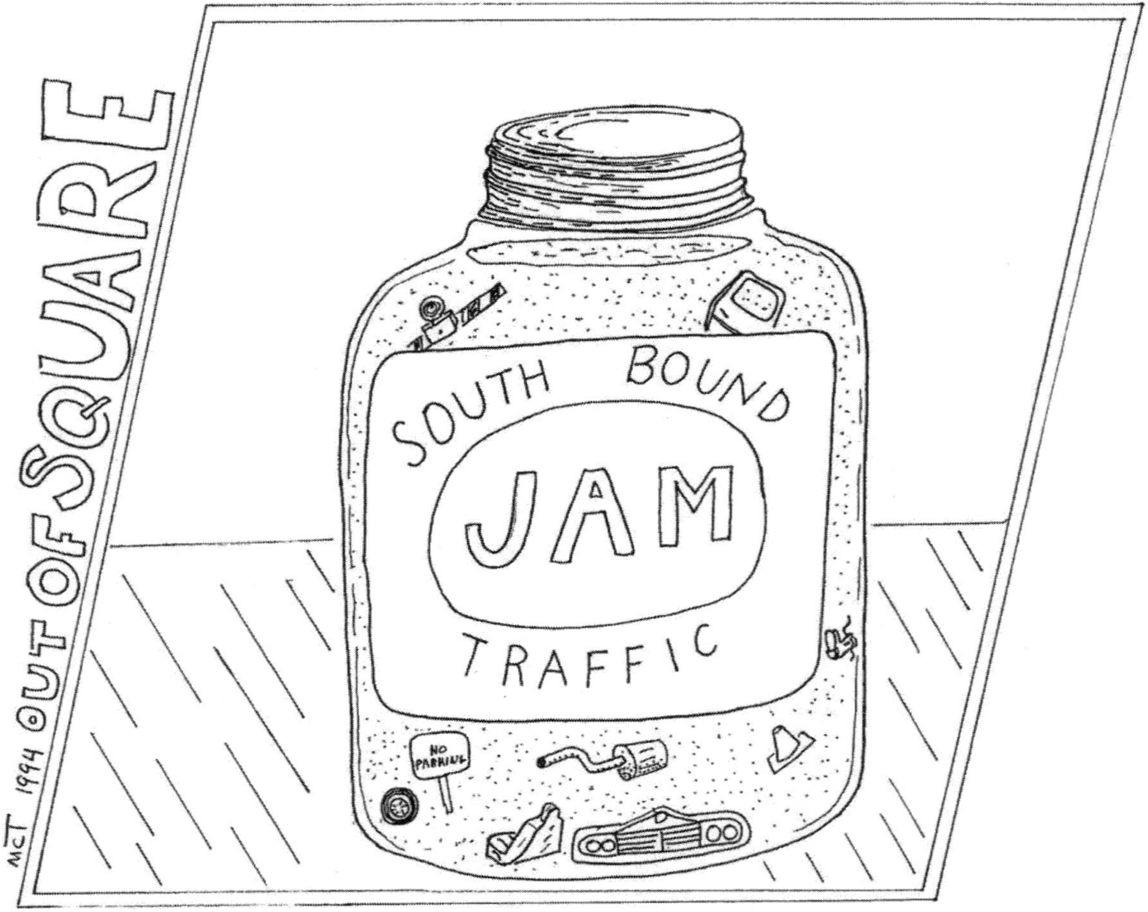
McT 1994 OUT OF SQUARE
SOUTH BOUND
JAM
TRAFFIC
NO PARKING

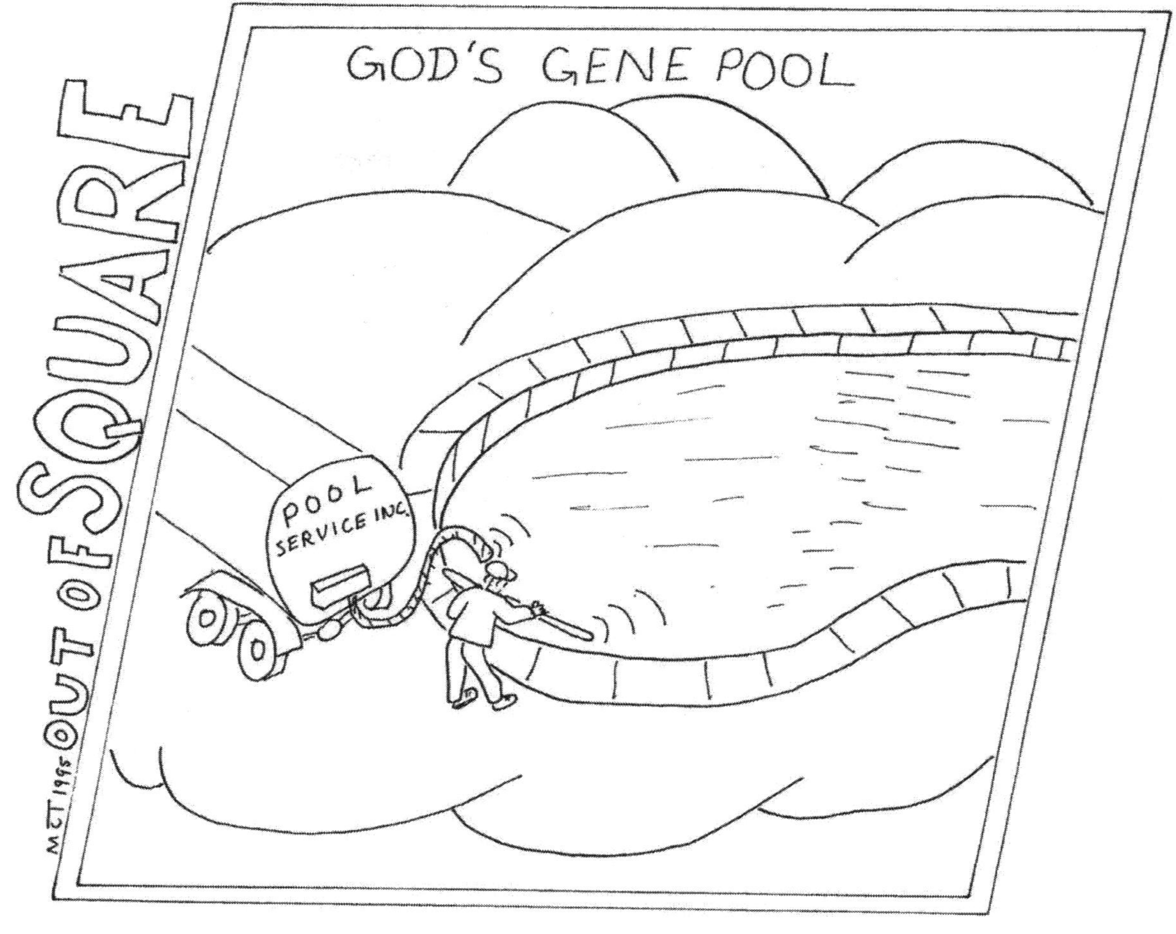
OUT OF SQUARE
GOD'S GENE POOL
POOL SERVICE INC.
MCT 1995

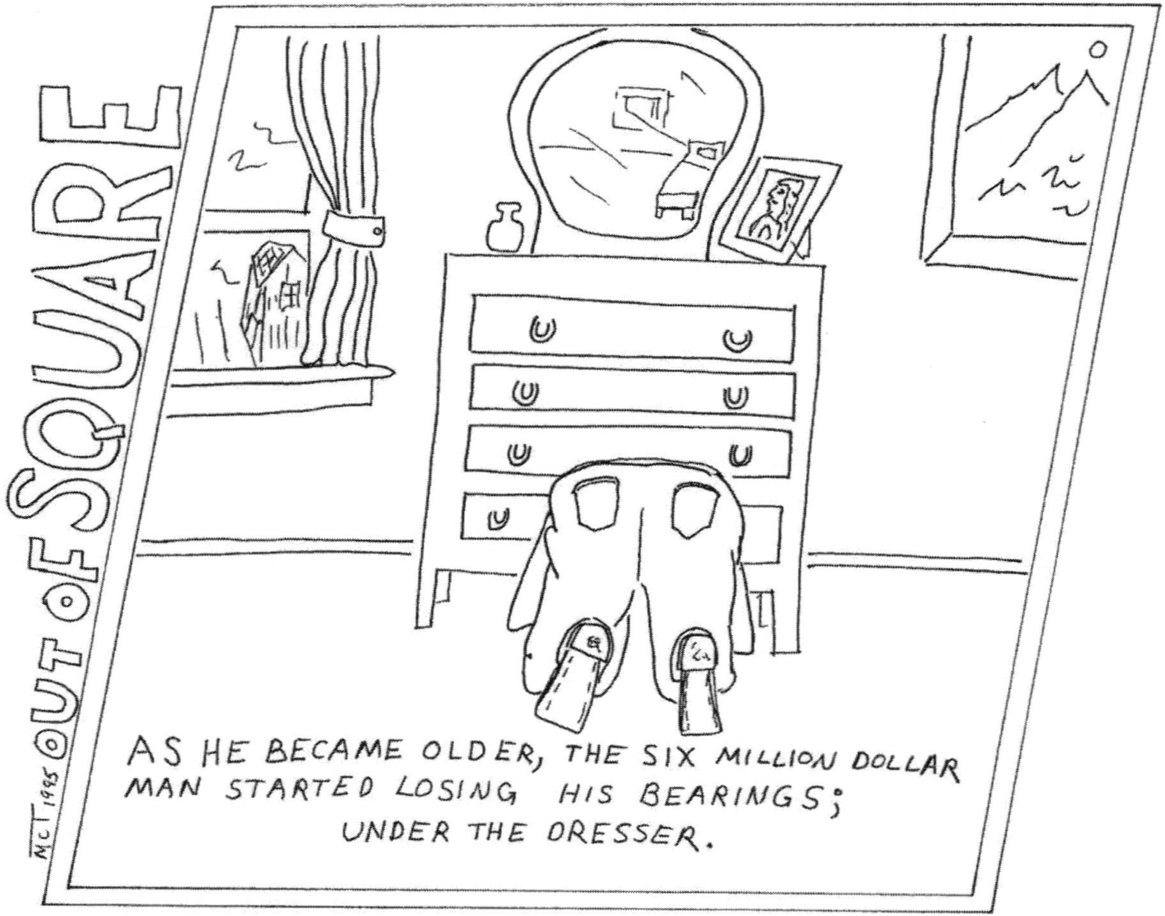
OUT OF SQUARE
MCT 1995
AS HE BECAME OLDER, THE SIX MILLION DOLLAR MAN STARTED LOSING HIS BEARINGS; UNDER THE DRESSER.

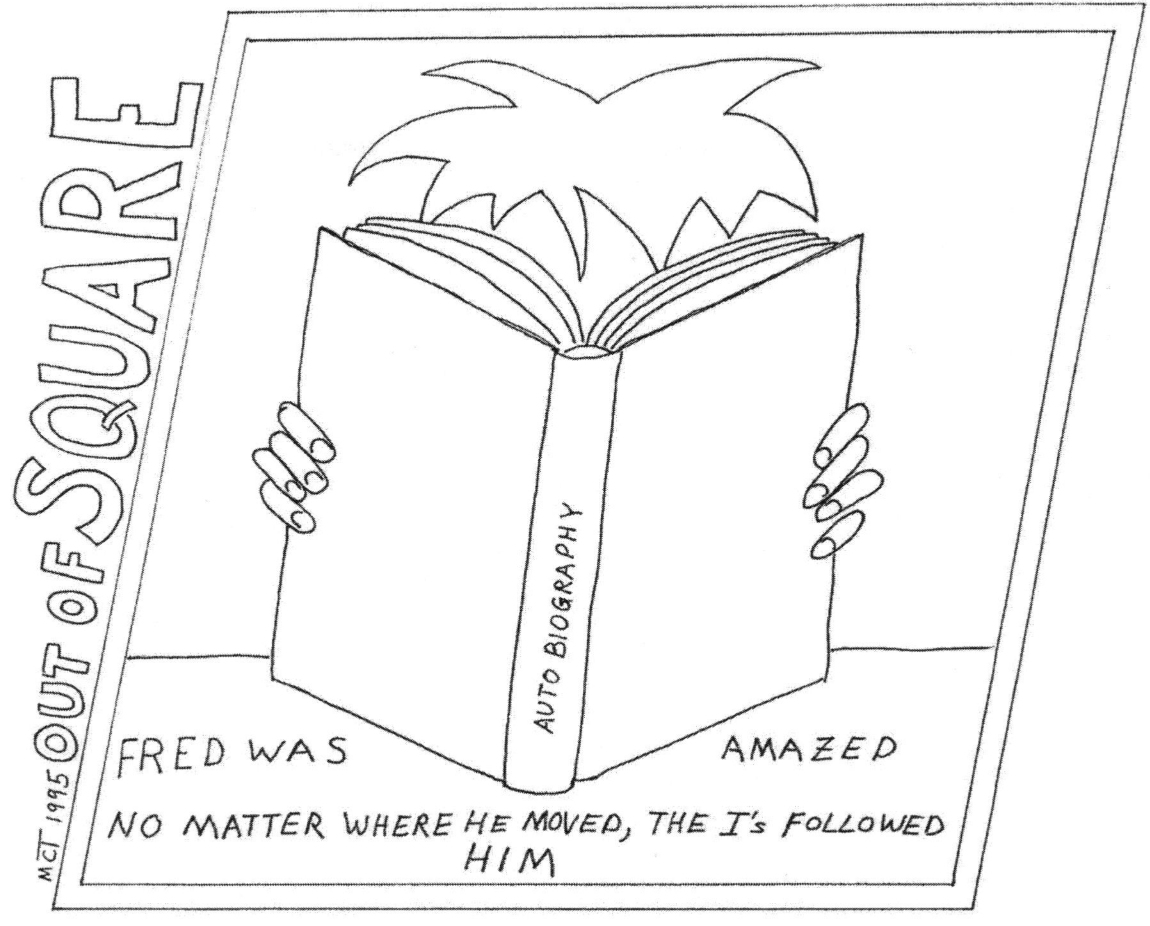
OUT OF SQUARE
MCT 1995
AUTO BIOGRAPHY
FRED WAS AMAZED
NO MATTER WHERE HE MOVED, THE I's FOLLOWED HIM

OUT OF SQUARE

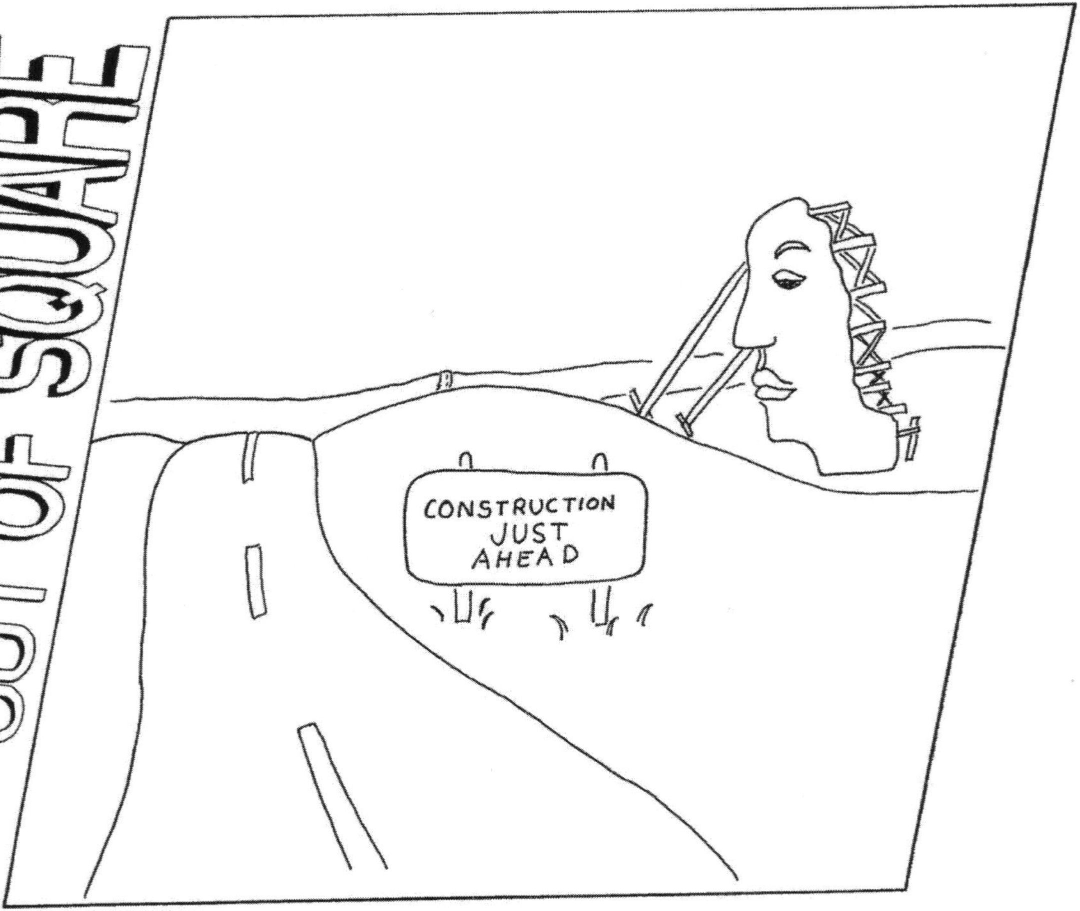
CONSTRUCTION
JUST
AHEAD

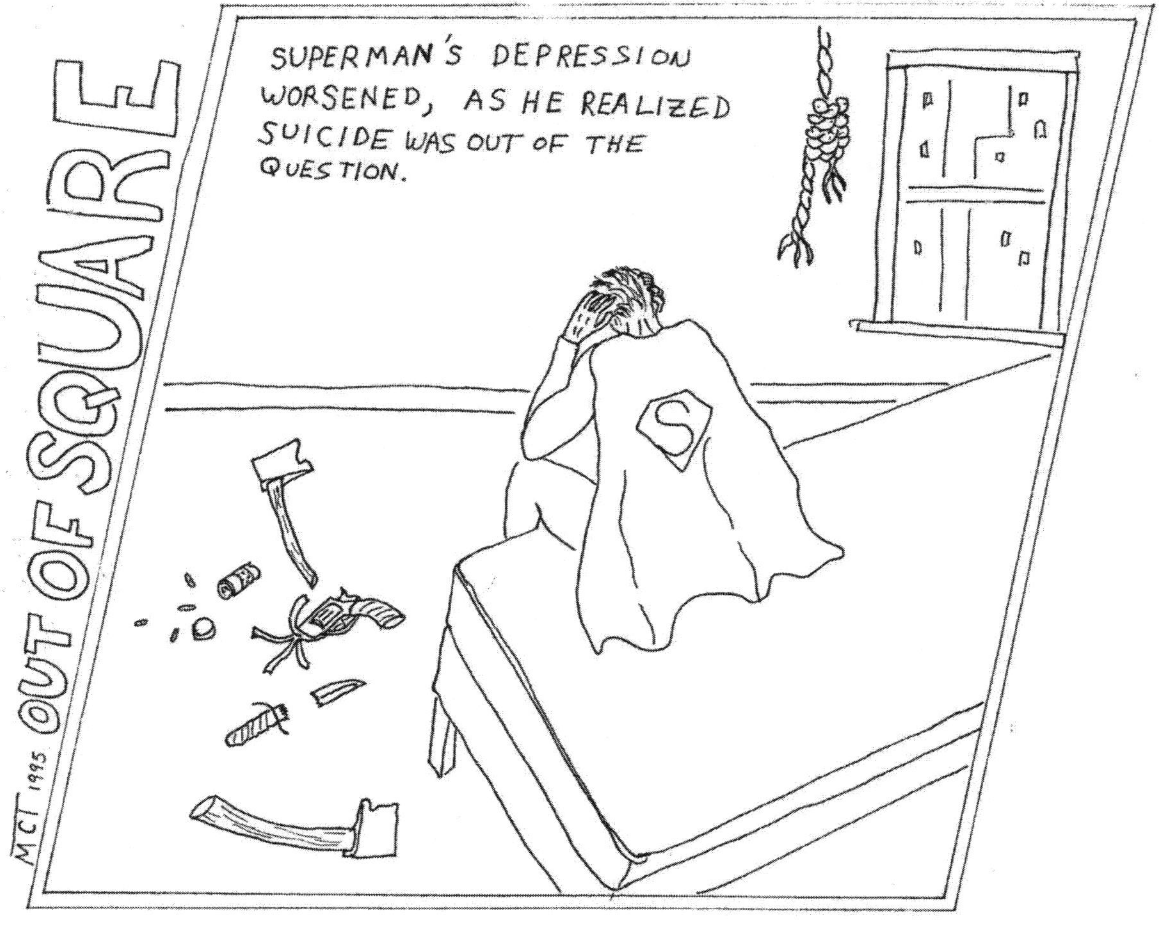
SUPERMAN'S DEPRESSION WORSENED, AS HE REALIZED SUICIDE WAS OUT OF THE QUESTION.
OUT OF SQUARE
MCT 1995
S

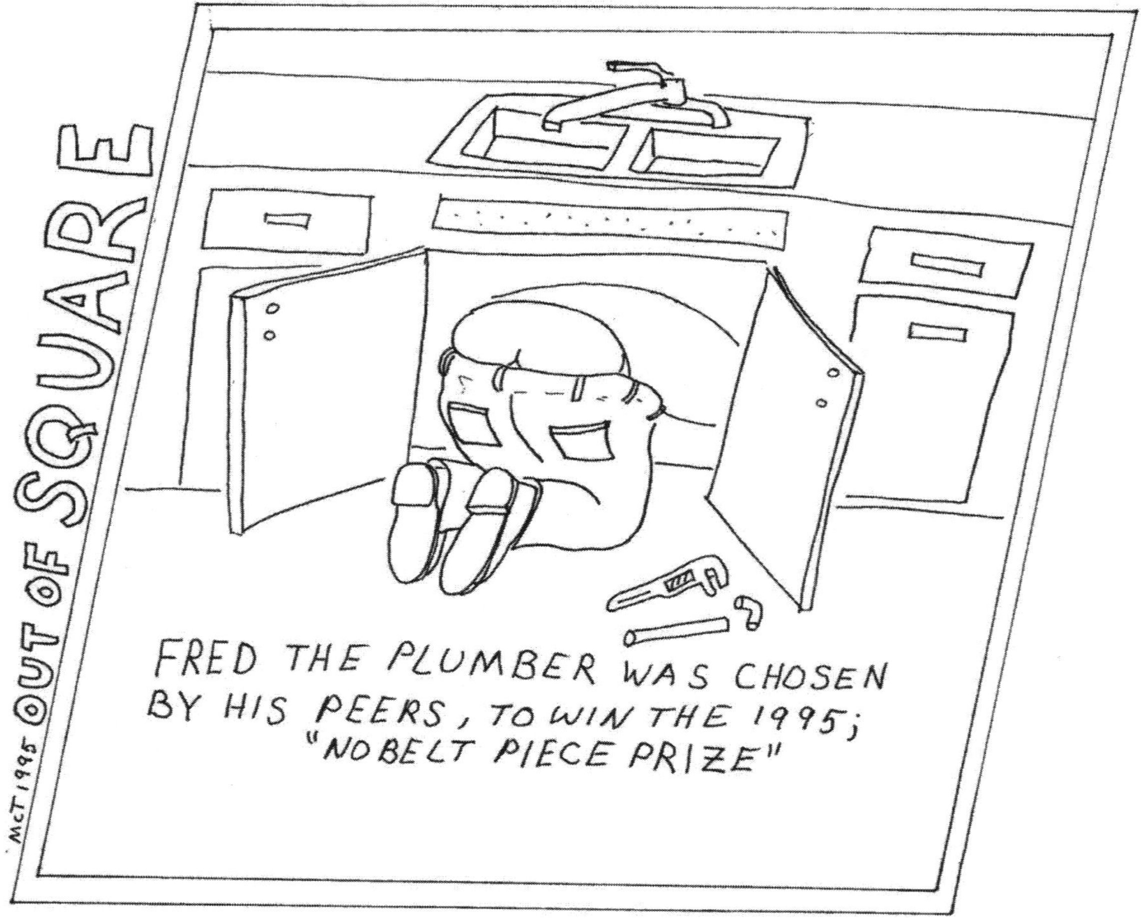
OUT OF SQUARE
McT 1995
FRED THE PLUMBER WAS CHOSEN
BY HIS PEERS, TO WIN THE 1995;
"NOBELT PIECE PRIZE"

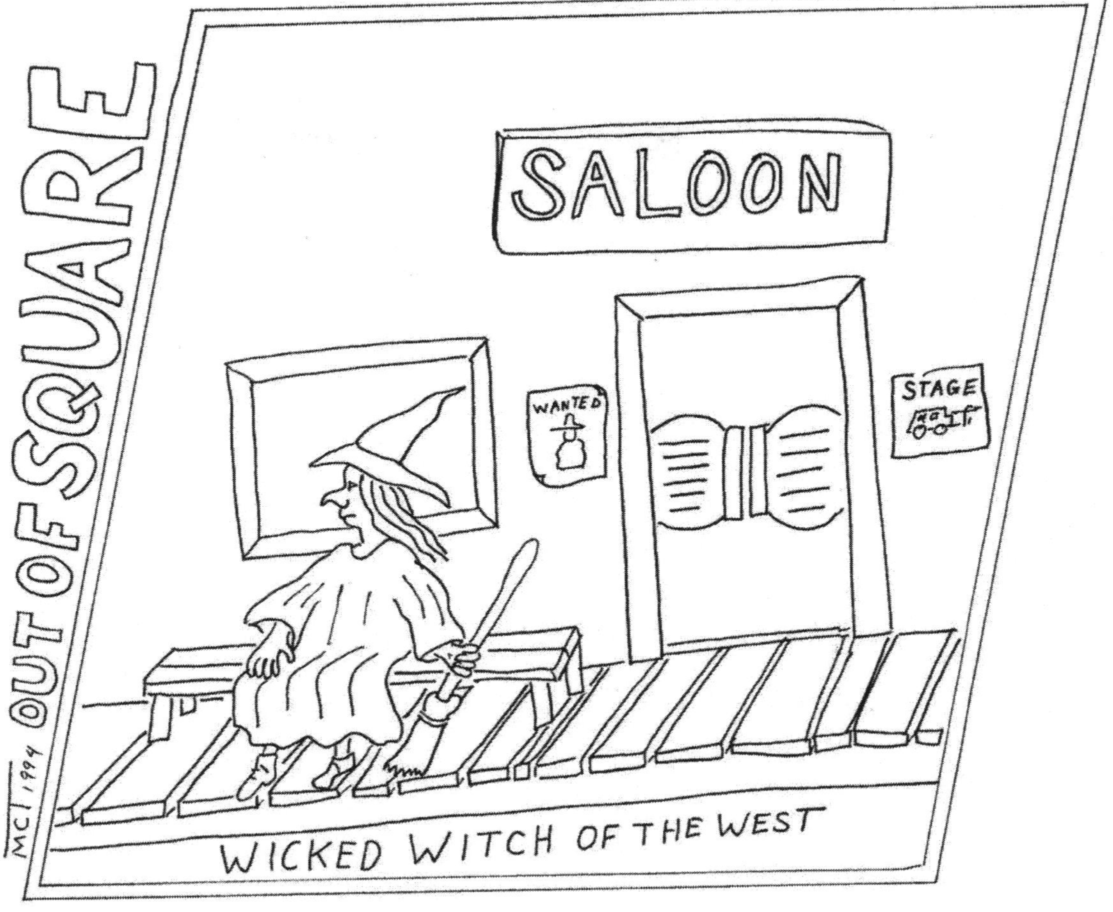
OUT OF SQUARE
MCI 1994
SALOON
WANTED
STAGE
WICKED WITCH OF THE WEST

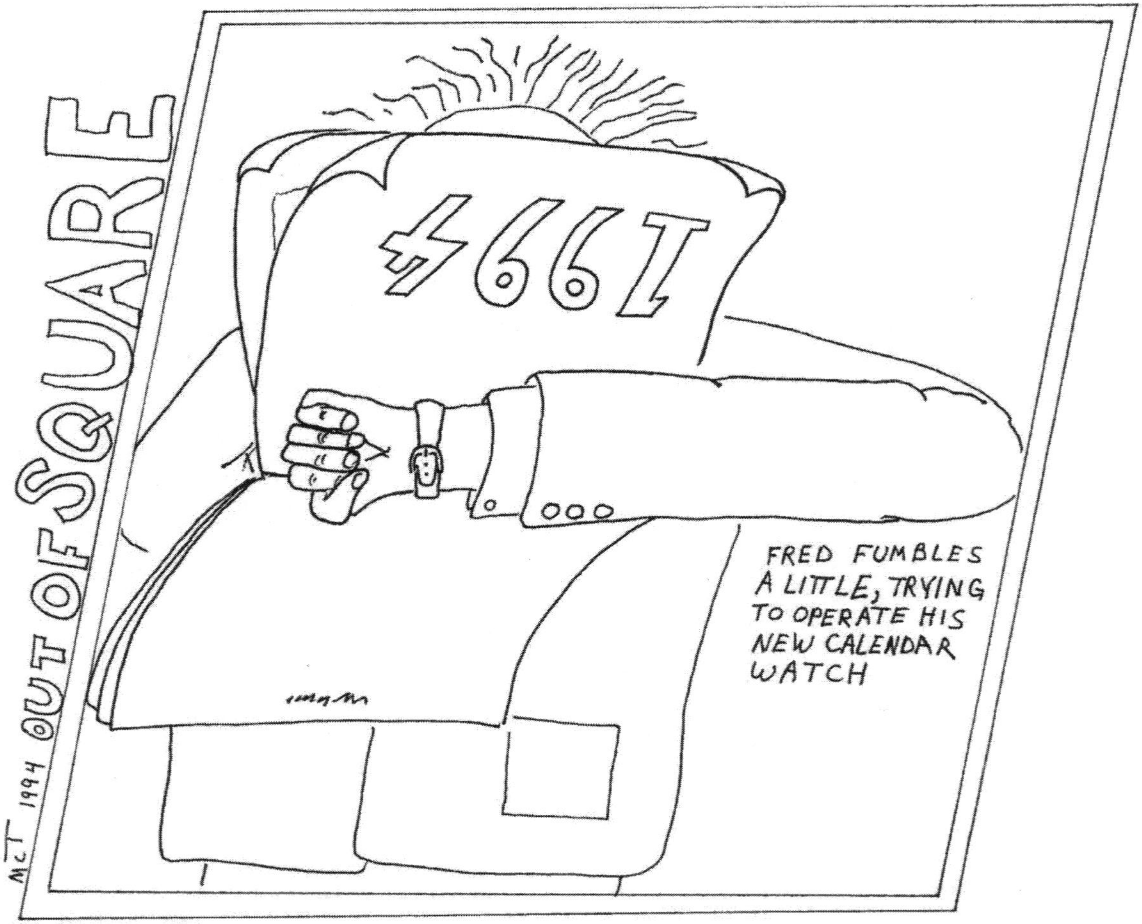
OUT OF SQUARE
McT 1994
FRED FUMBLES A LITTLE, TRYING TO OPERATE HIS NEW CALENDAR WATCH

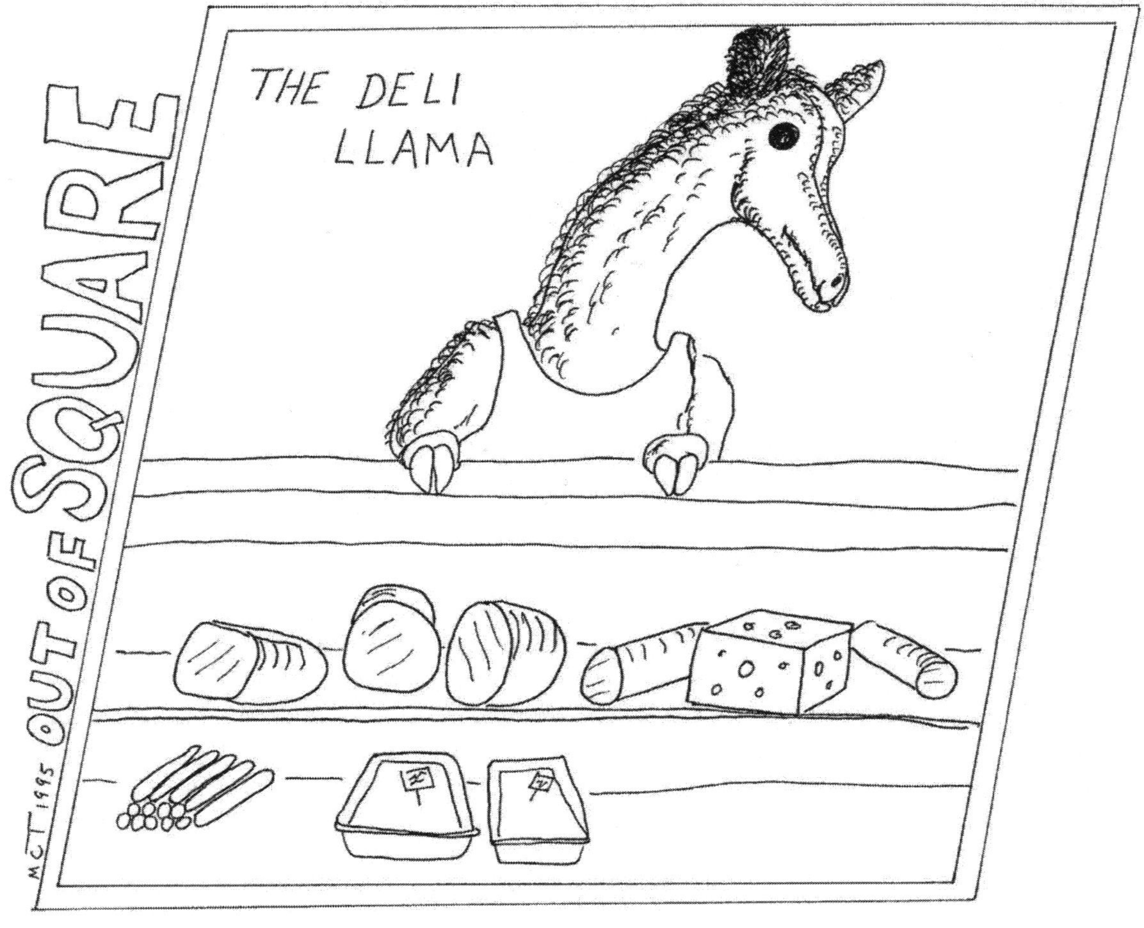
OUT OF SQUARE
THE DELI LLAMA
MCT 1995

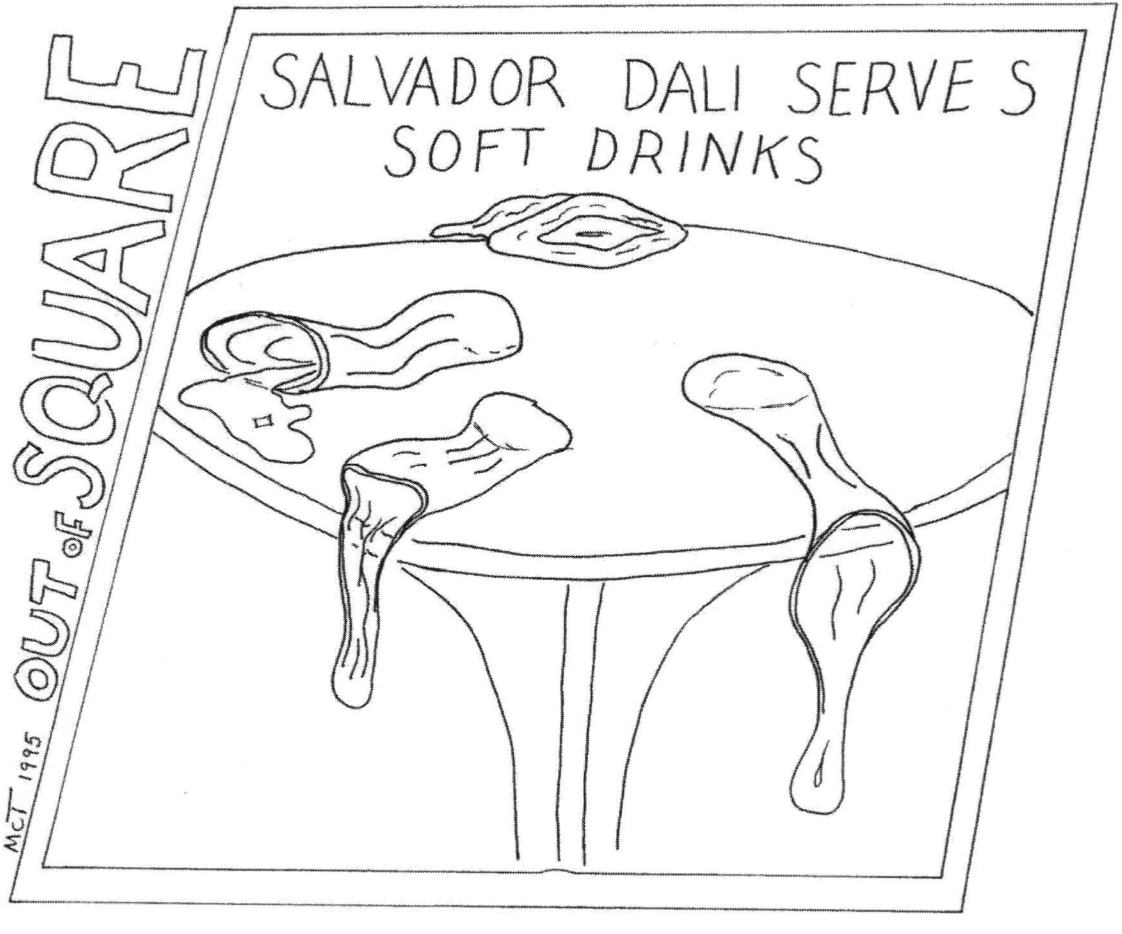
OUT of SQUARE
SALVADOR DALI SERVES
SOFT DRINKS
McT 1995

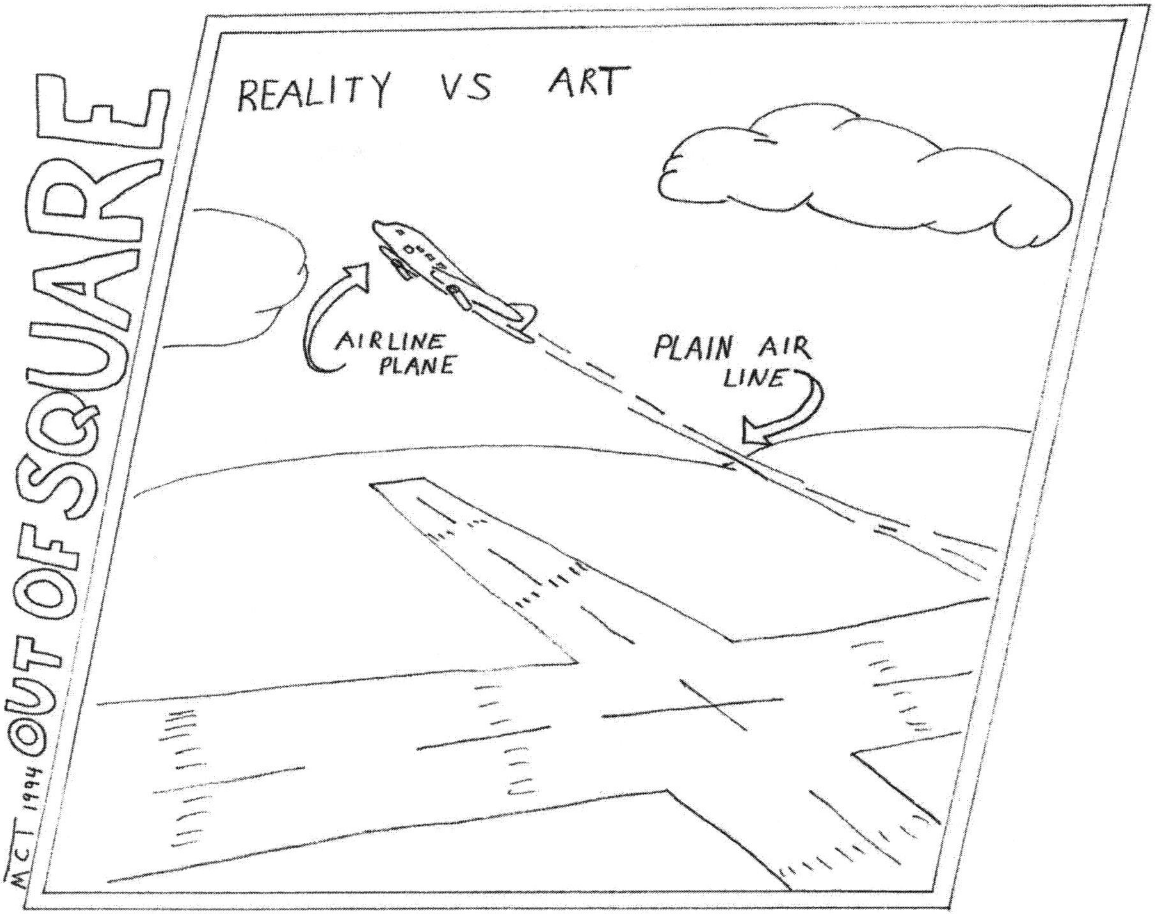
OUT OF SQUARE
MCT 1994
REALITY VS ART
AIRLINE PLANE
PLAIN AIR LINE

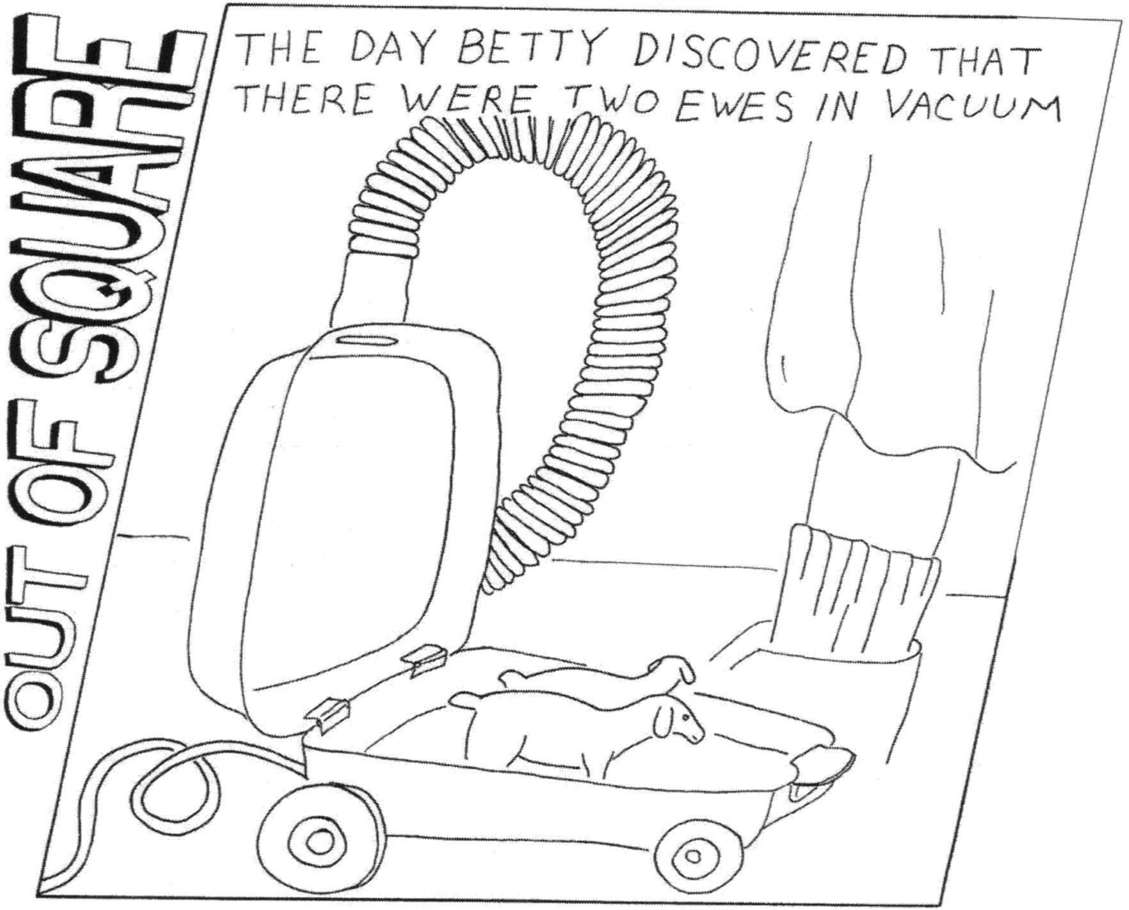
OUT OF SQUARE
THE DAY BETTY DISCOVERED THAT THERE WERE TWO EWES IN VACUUM

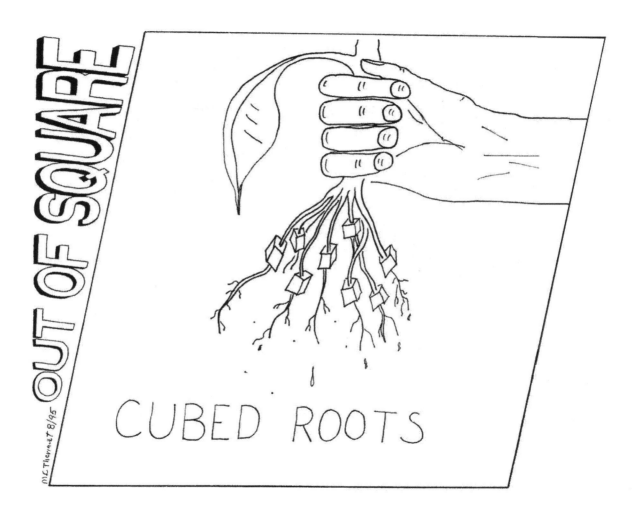

OUT OF SQUARE

CUBED ROOTS

M.C.Theriault 8/95

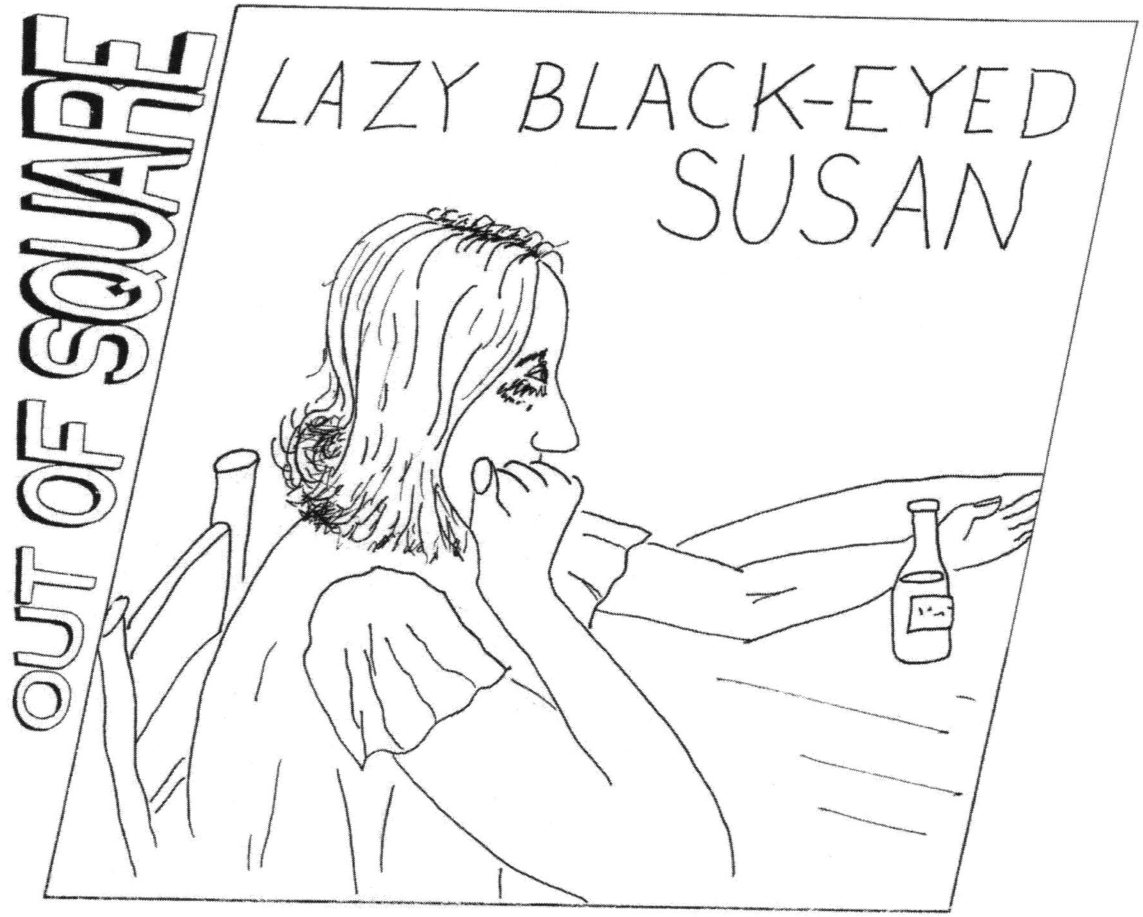
OUT OF SQUARE
LAZY BLACK-EYED
SUSAN

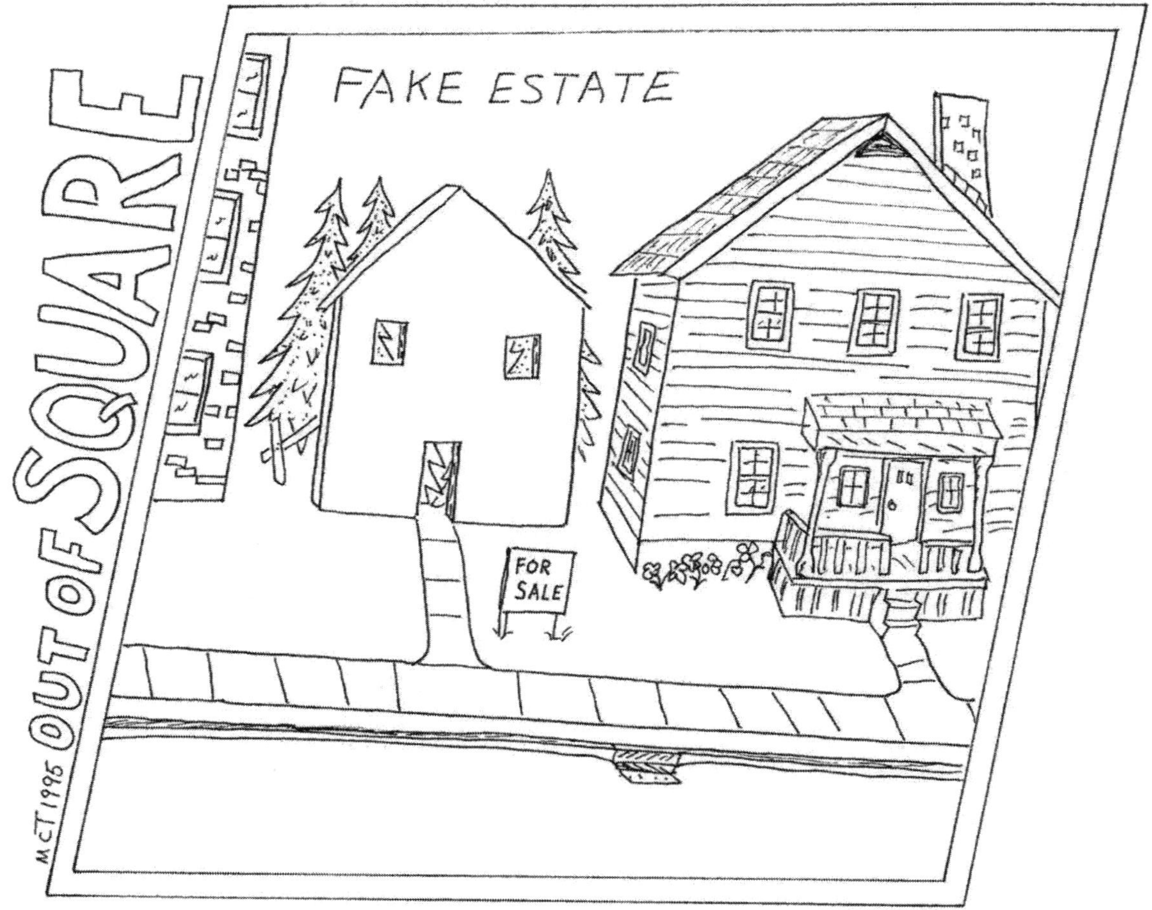
MCT 1995 OUT OF SQUARE
FAKE ESTATE
FOR SALE

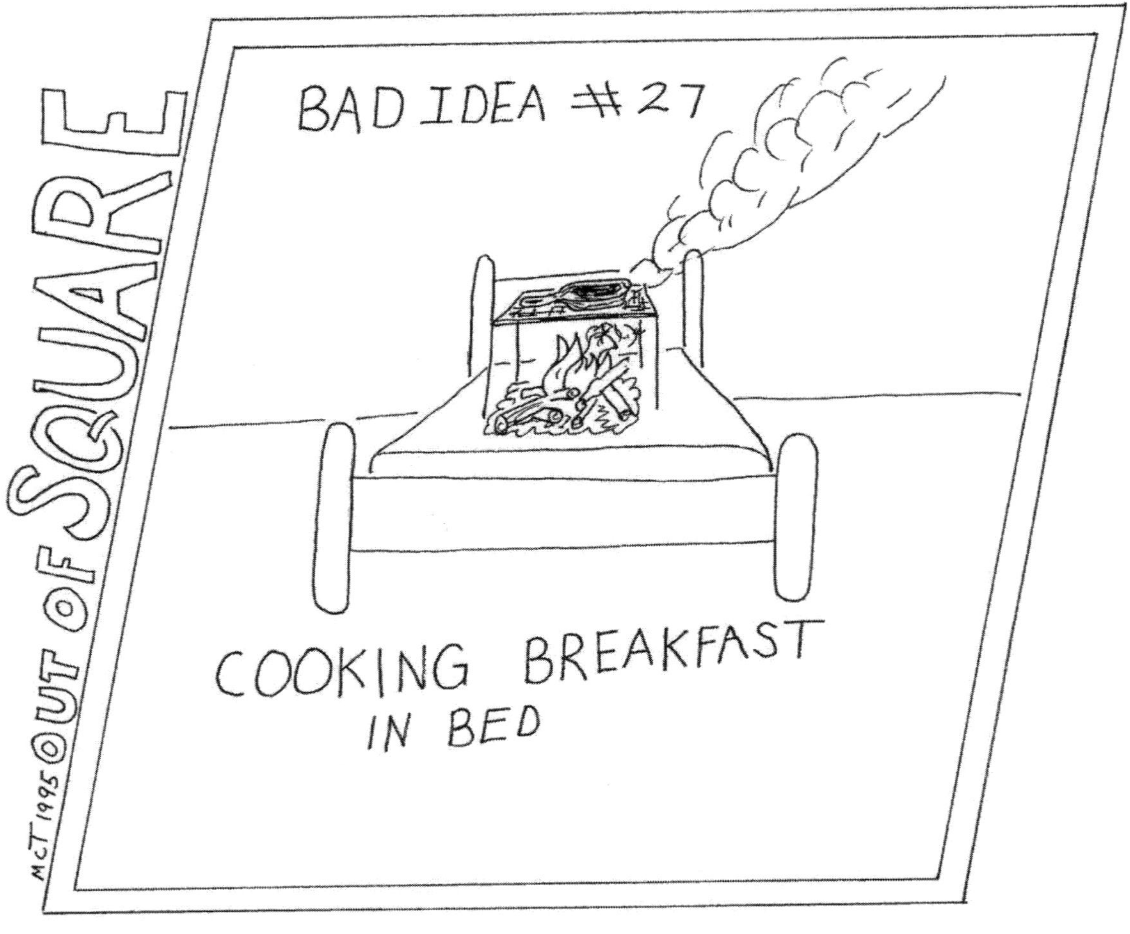
OUT OF SQUARE
McT 1995
BAD IDEA #27
COOKING BREAKFAST IN BED

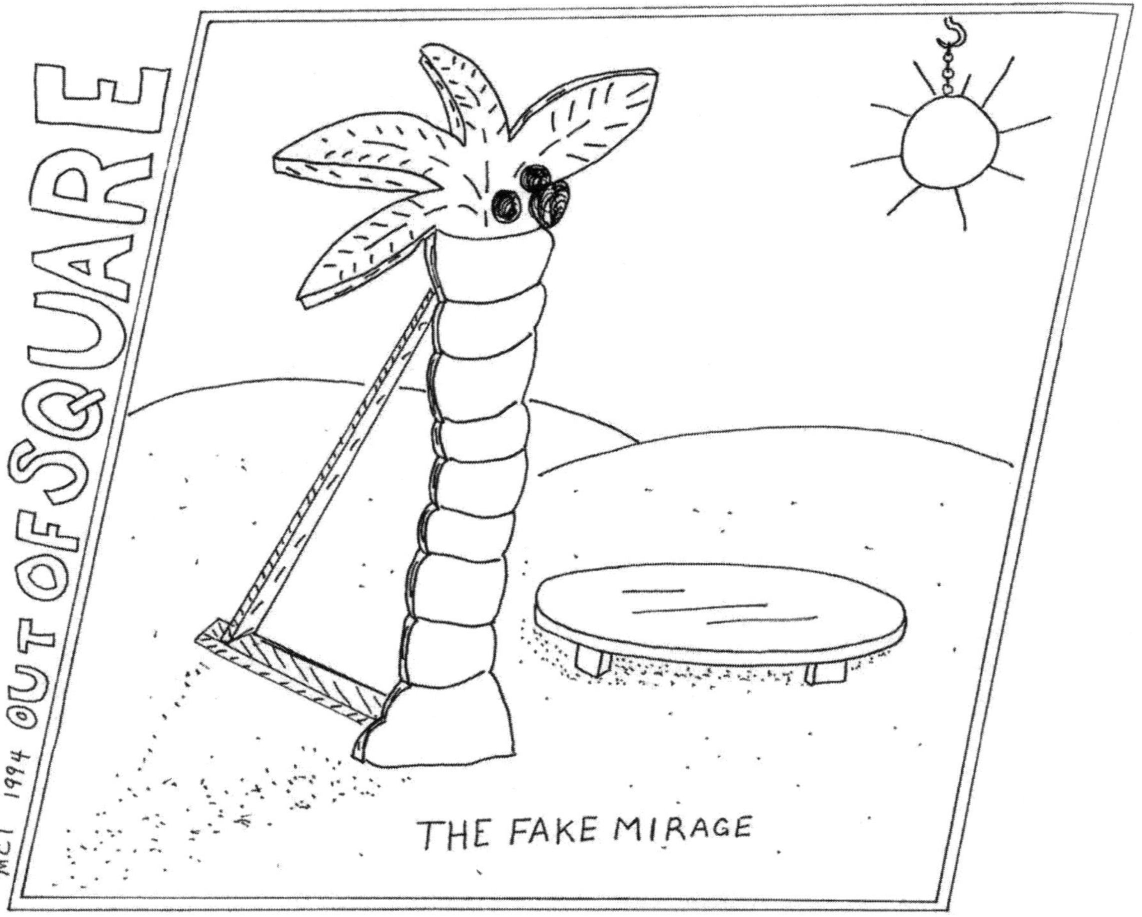
OUT OF SQUARE
MCT 1994
THE FAKE MIRAGE

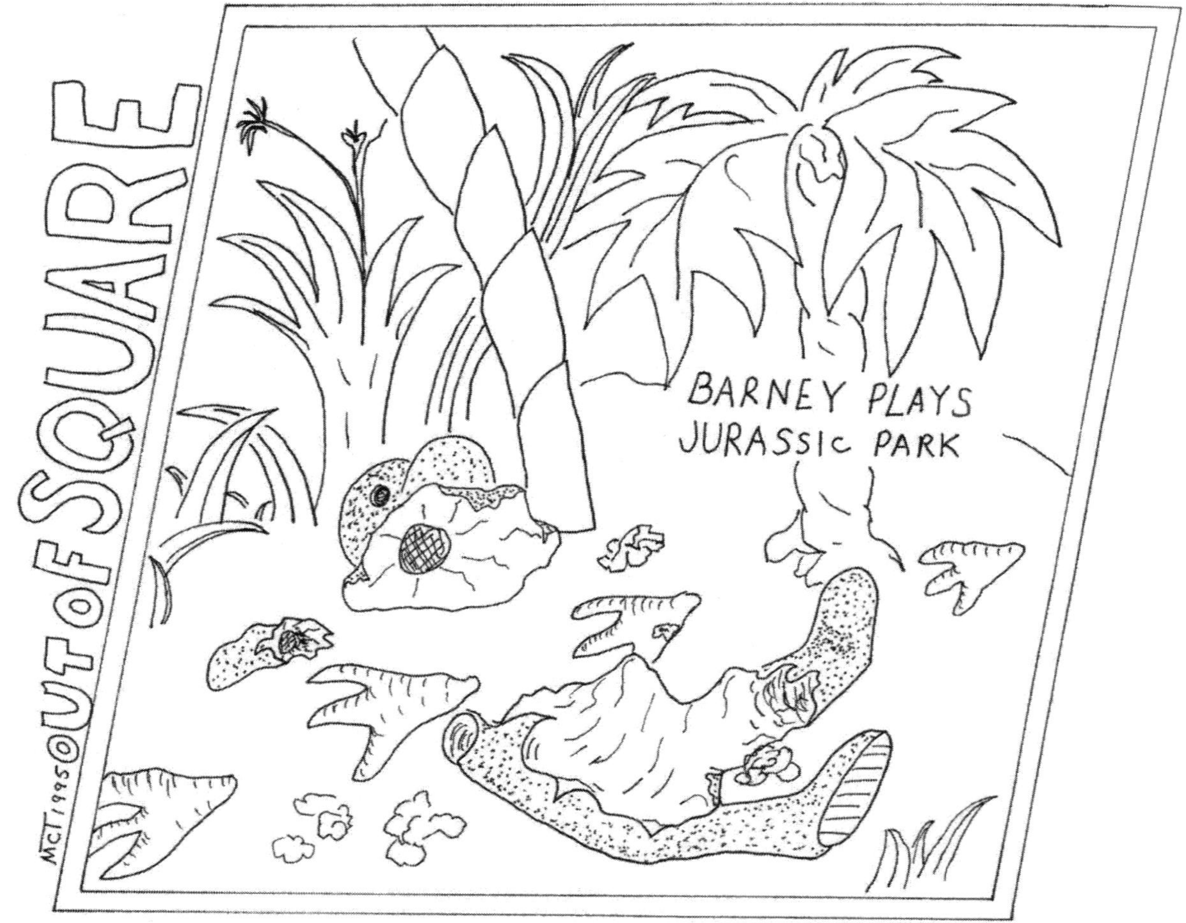
OUT OF SQUARE
MCT 1995
BARNEY PLAYS
JURASSIC PARK

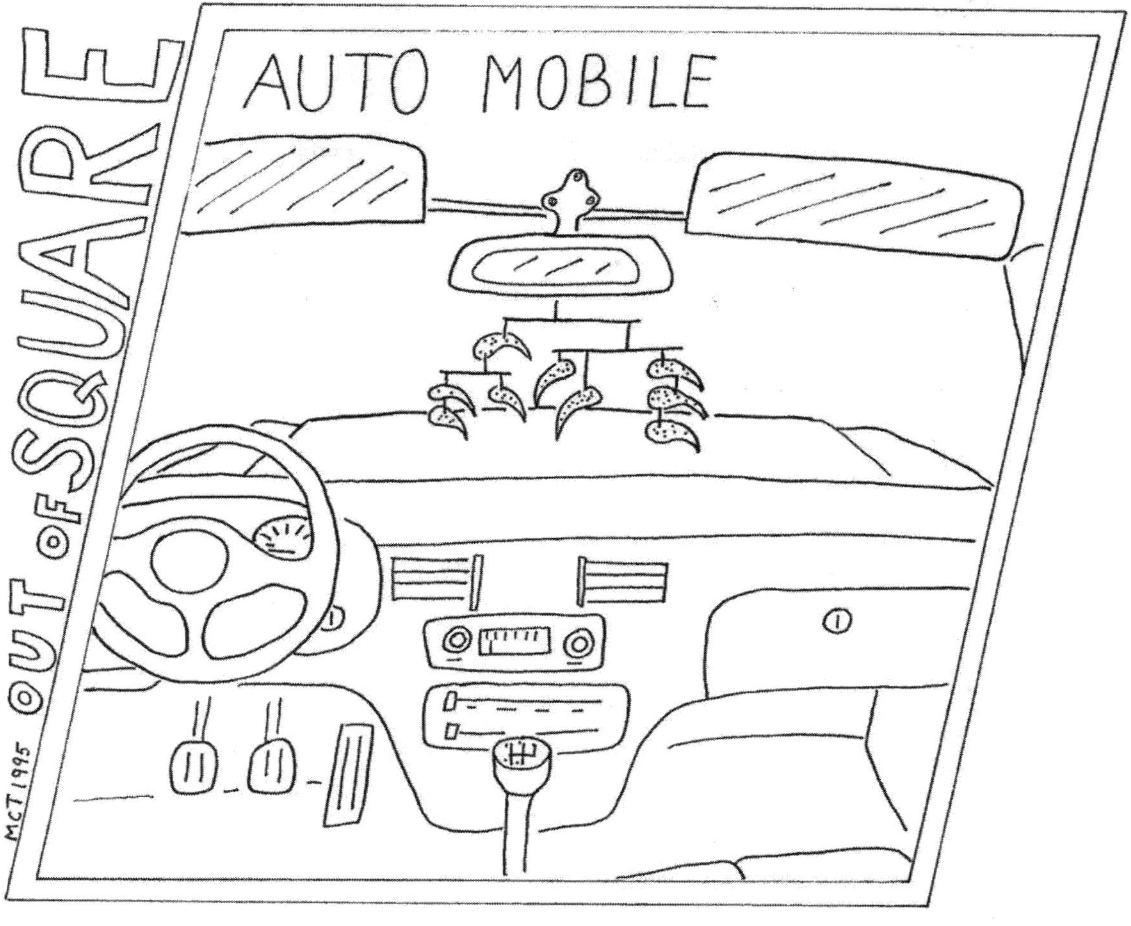
OUT of SQUARE
AUTO MOBILE
MCT 1995

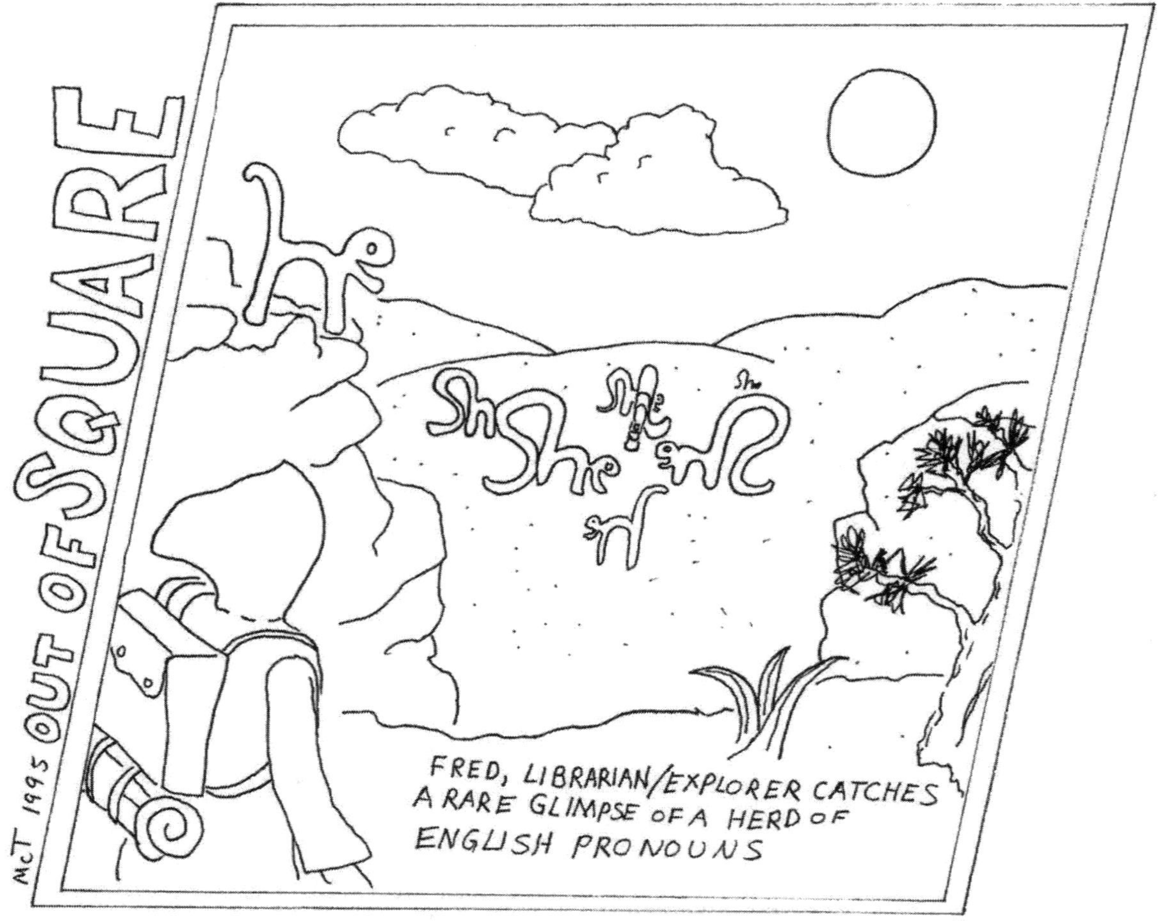

OUT OF SQUARE
McT 1995
FRED, LIBRARIAN/EXPLORER CATCHES A RARE GLIMPSE OF A HERD OF ENGLISH PRONOUNS

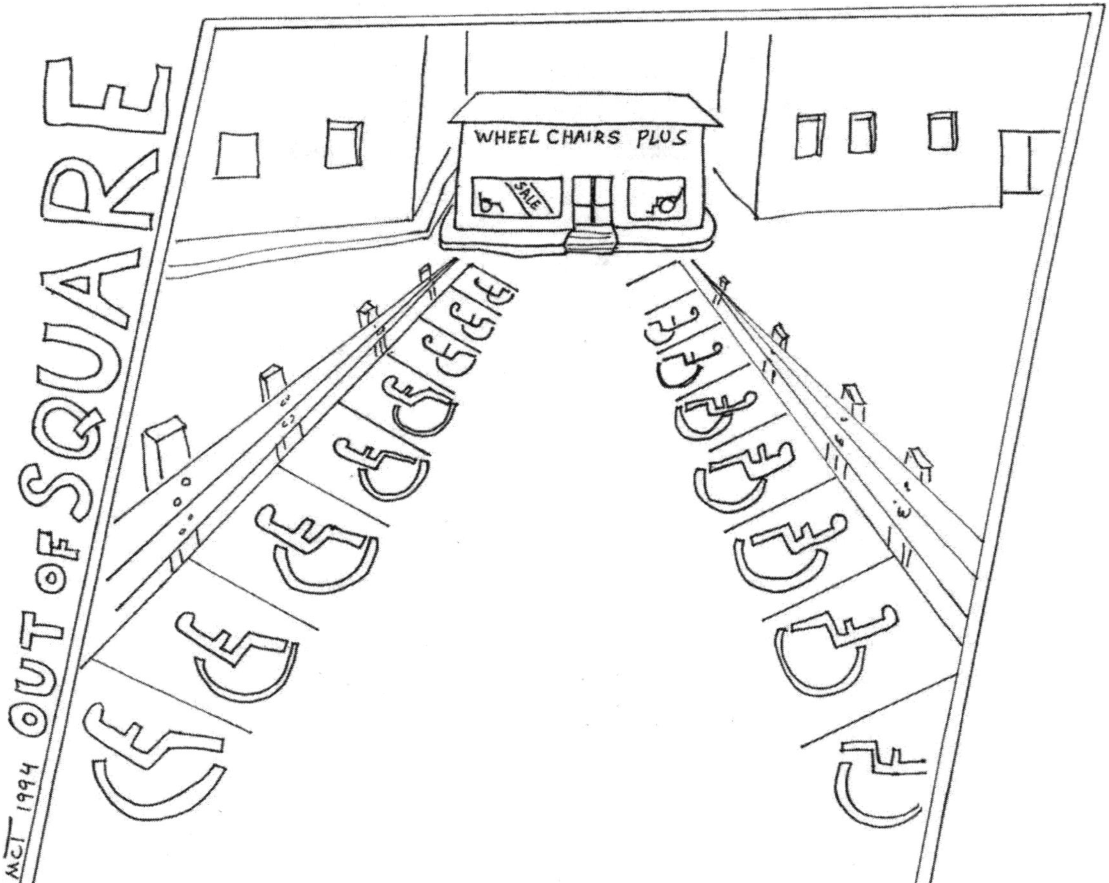
WHEEL CHAIRS PLUS
SALE
OUT OF SQUARE
MCT 1994

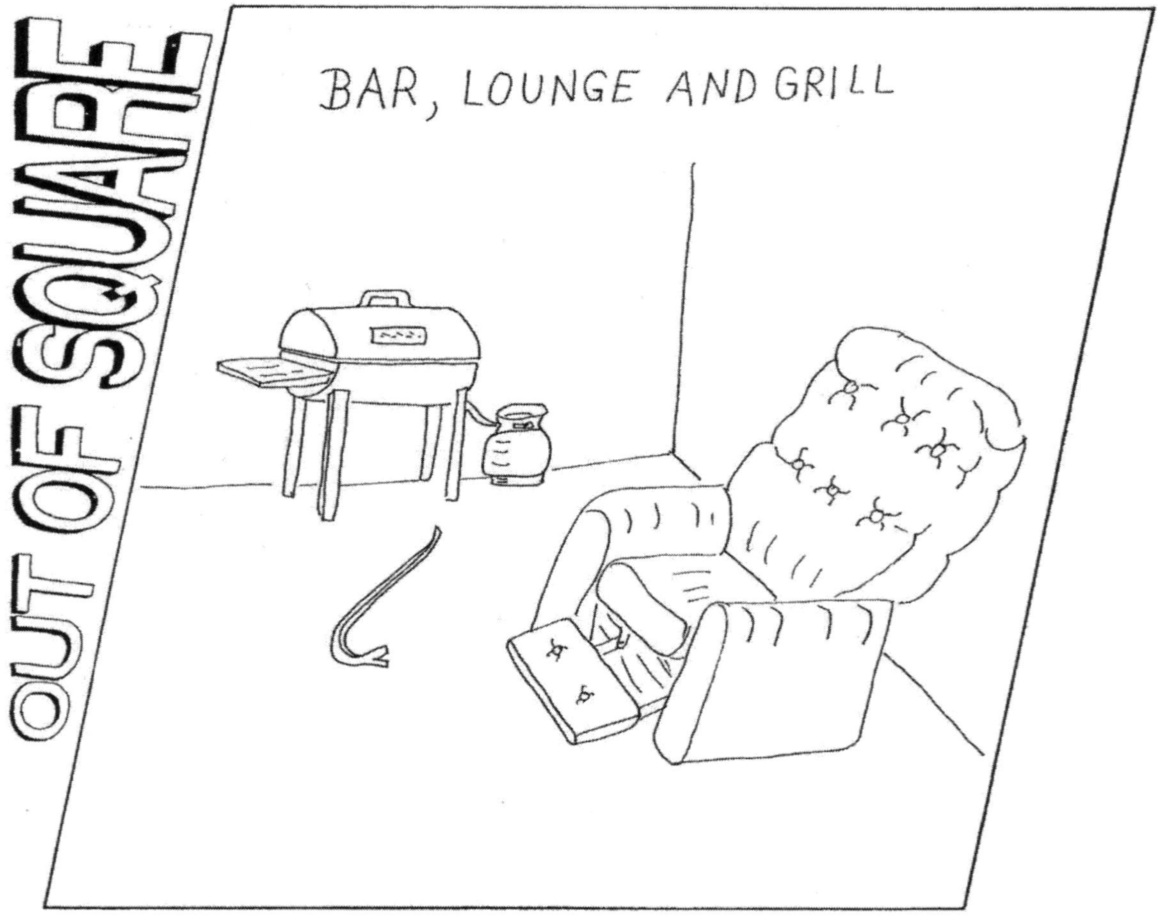
OUT OF SQUARE
BAR, LOUNGE AND GRILL

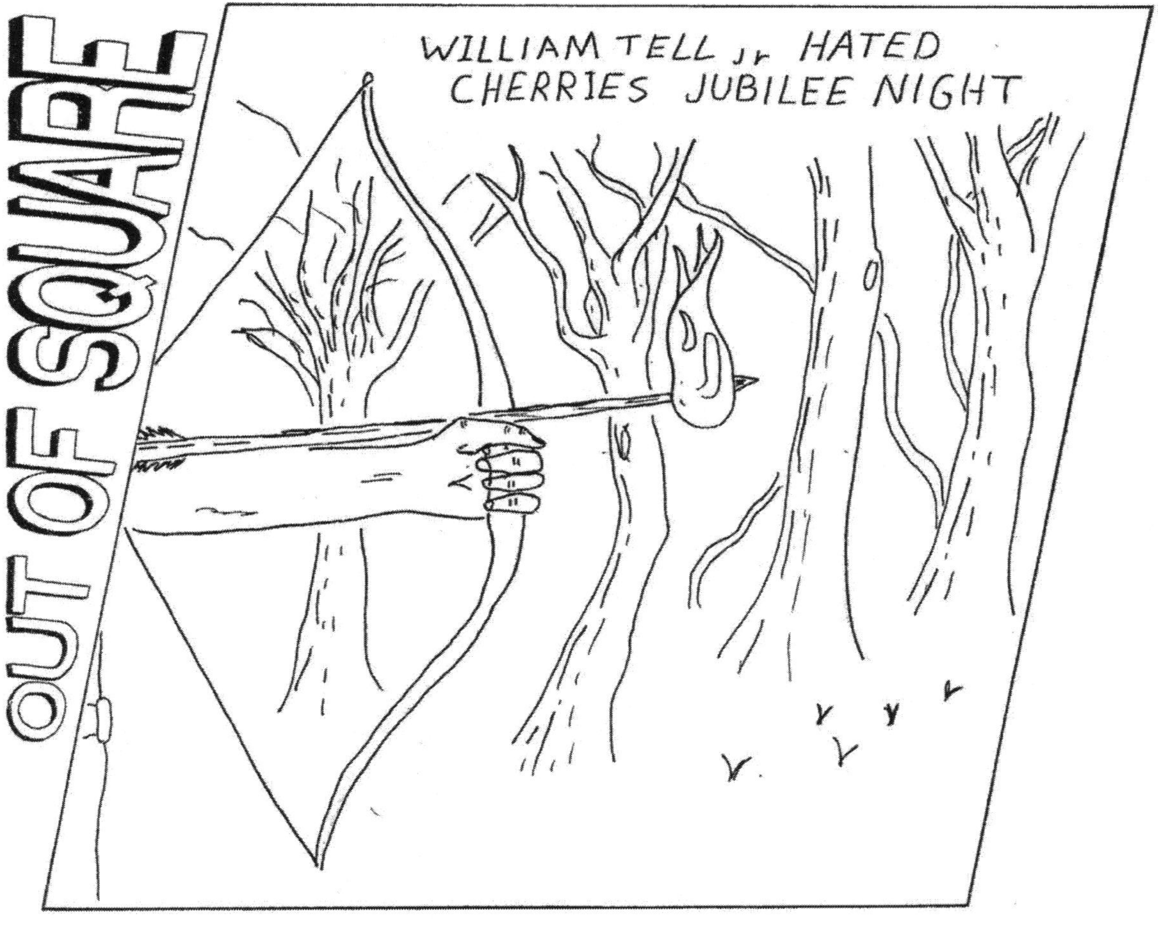
OUT OF SQUARE
WILLIAM TELL jr HATED
CHERRIES JUBILEE NIGHT

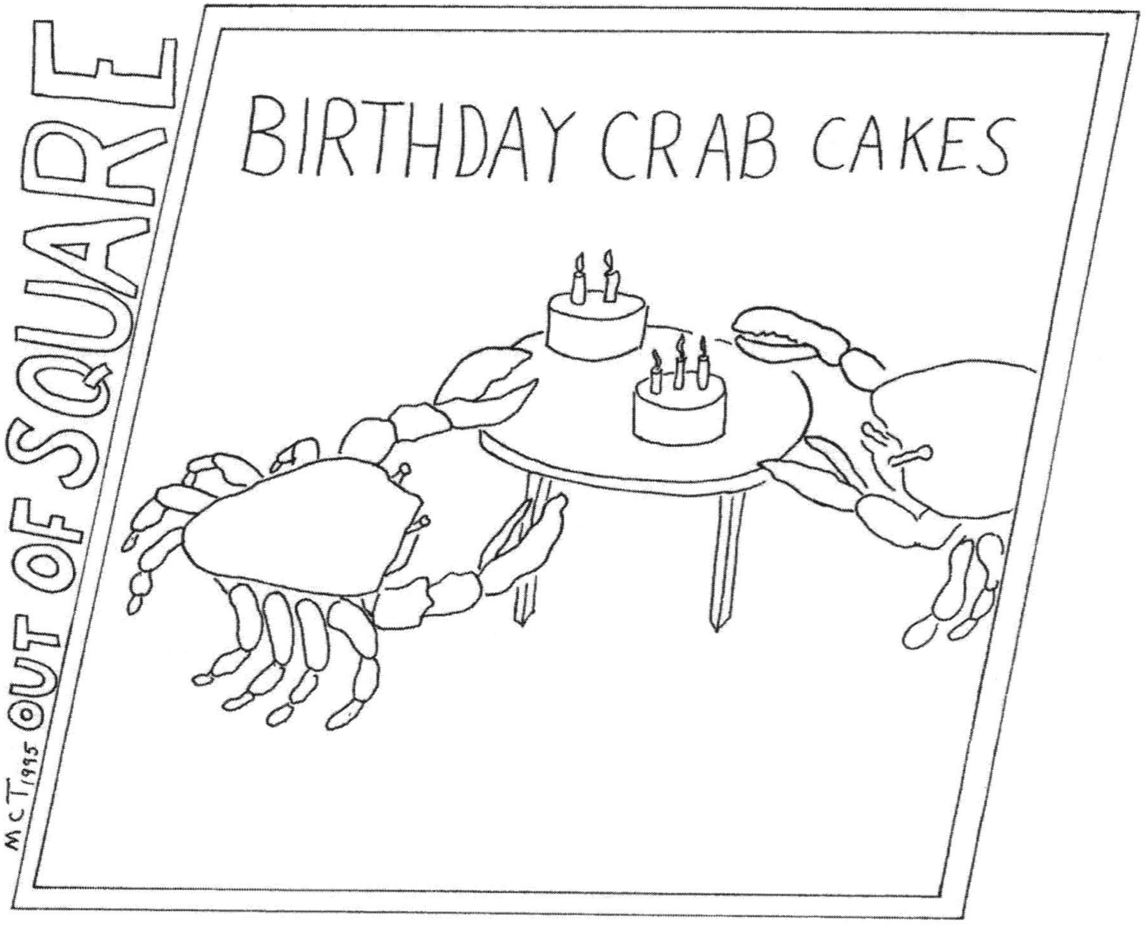
OUT OF SQUARE
BIRTHDAY CRAB CAKES
© MCT 1995

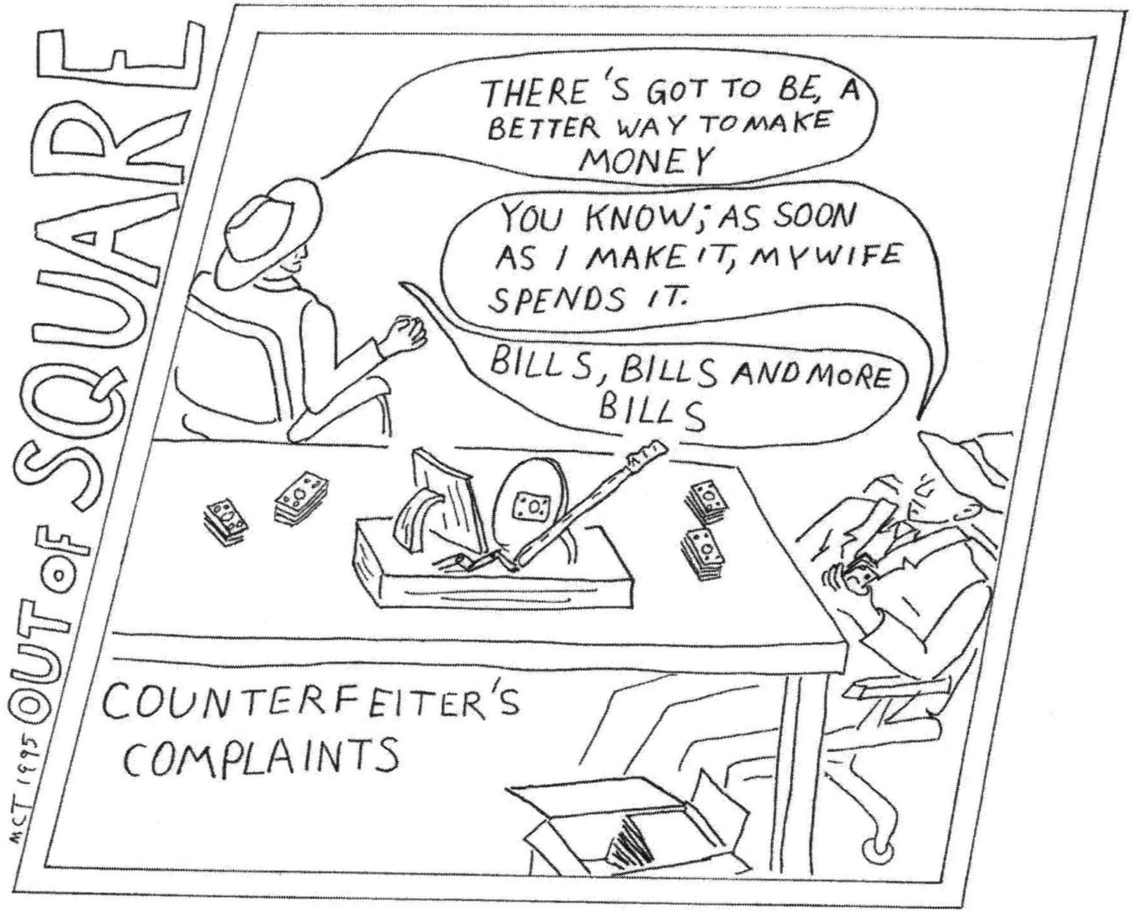
OUT OF SQUARE
MCT 1995
THERE'S GOT TO BE, A BETTER WAY TO MAKE MONEY
YOU KNOW; AS SOON AS I MAKE IT, MY WIFE SPENDS IT.
BILLS, BILLS AND MORE BILLS
COUNTERFEITER'S COMPLAINTS

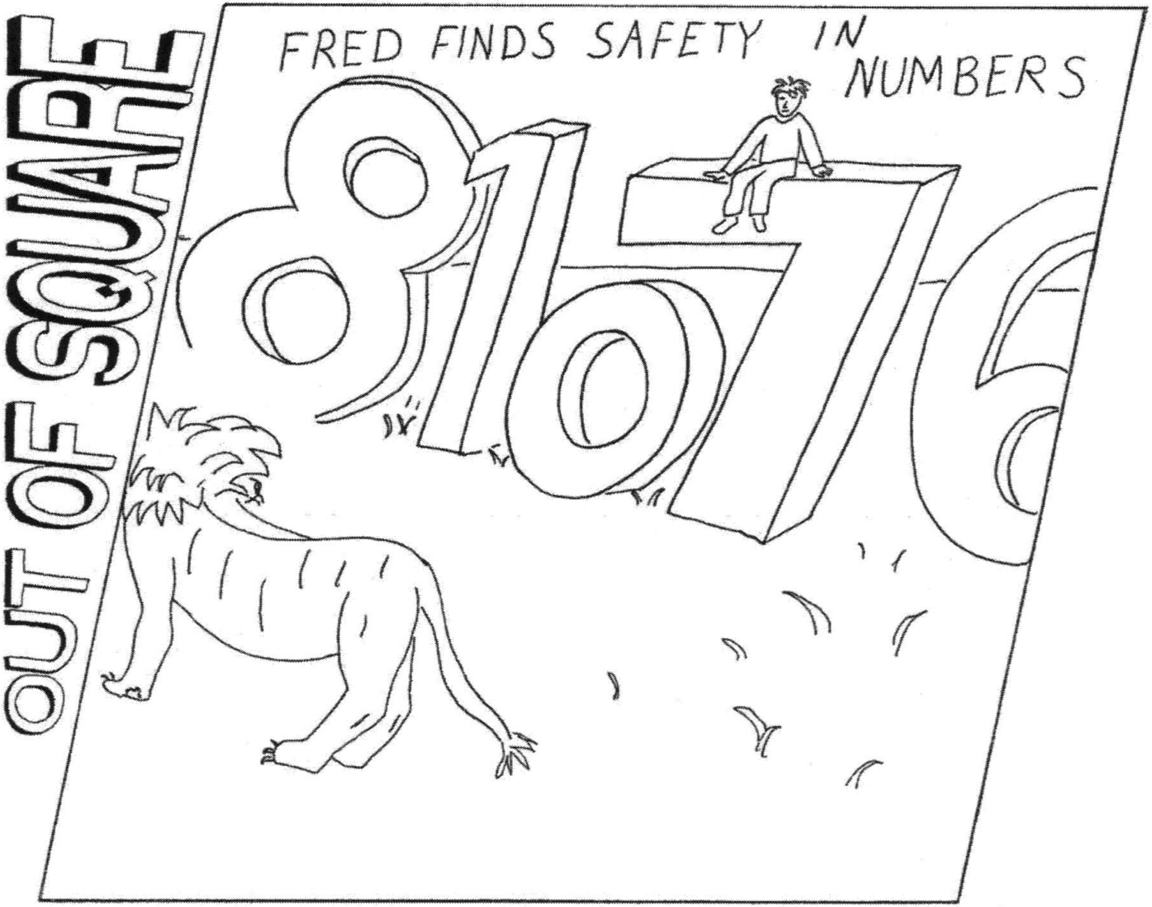
OUT OF SQUARE
FRED FINDS SAFETY IN NUMBERS
8176

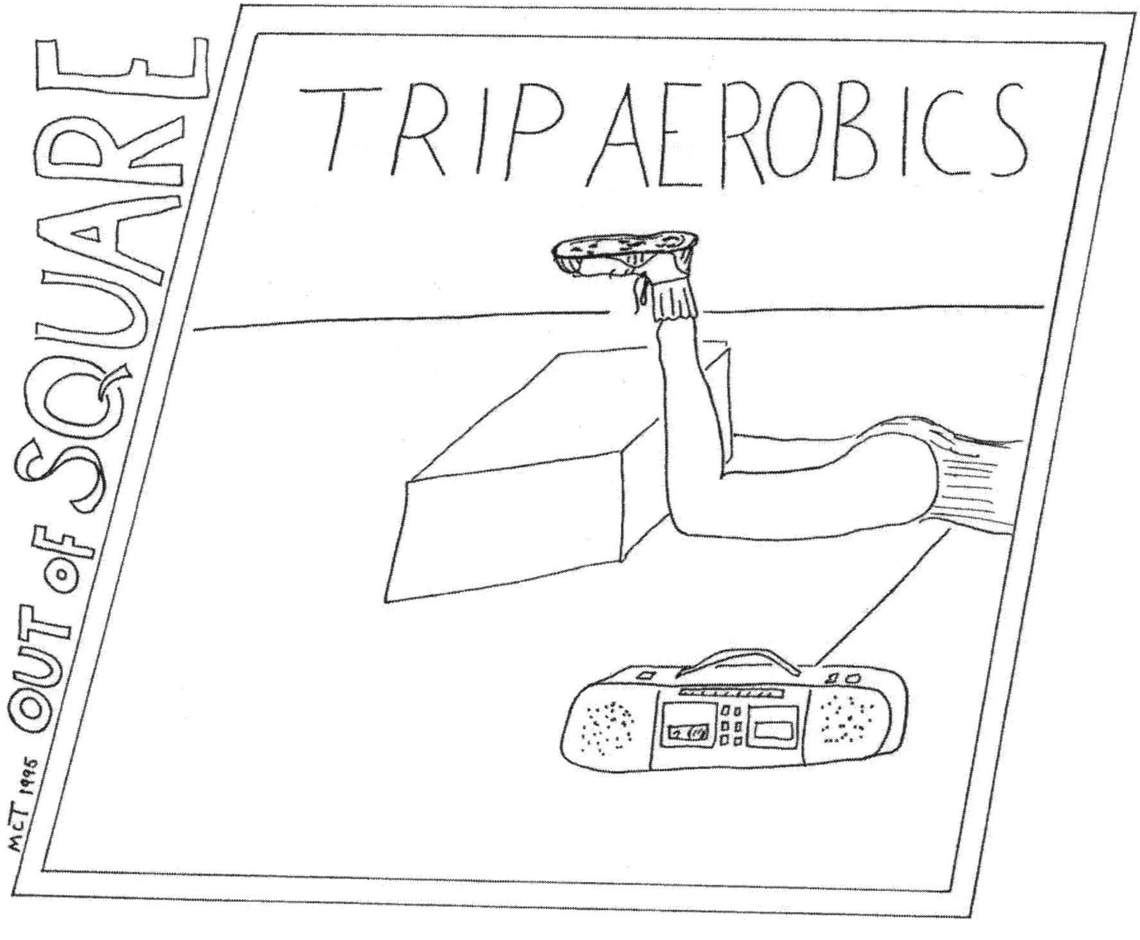
OUT of SQUARE
TRIP AEROBICS
MCT 1995

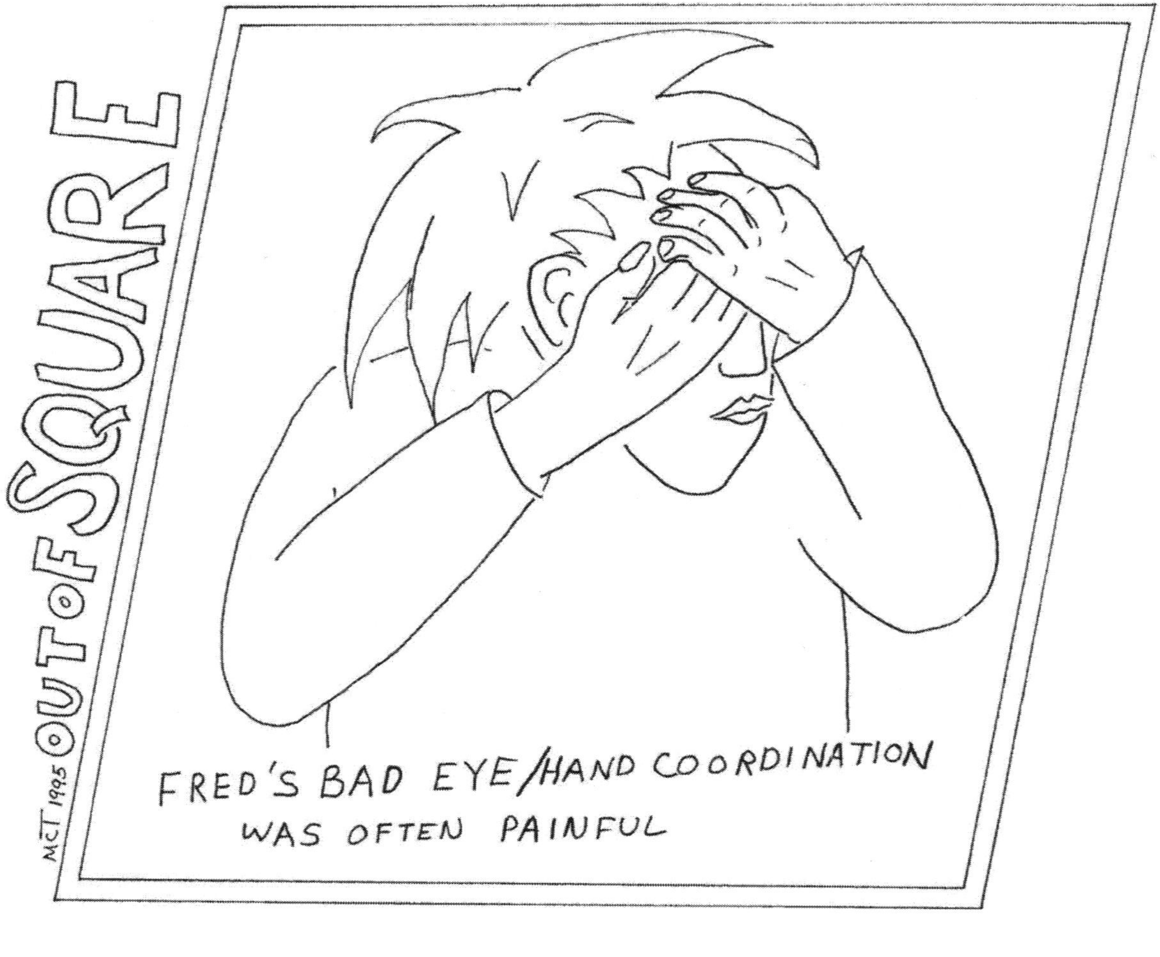
OUT OF SQUARE
MCT 1995
FRED'S BAD EYE/HAND COORDINATION
WAS OFTEN PAINFUL

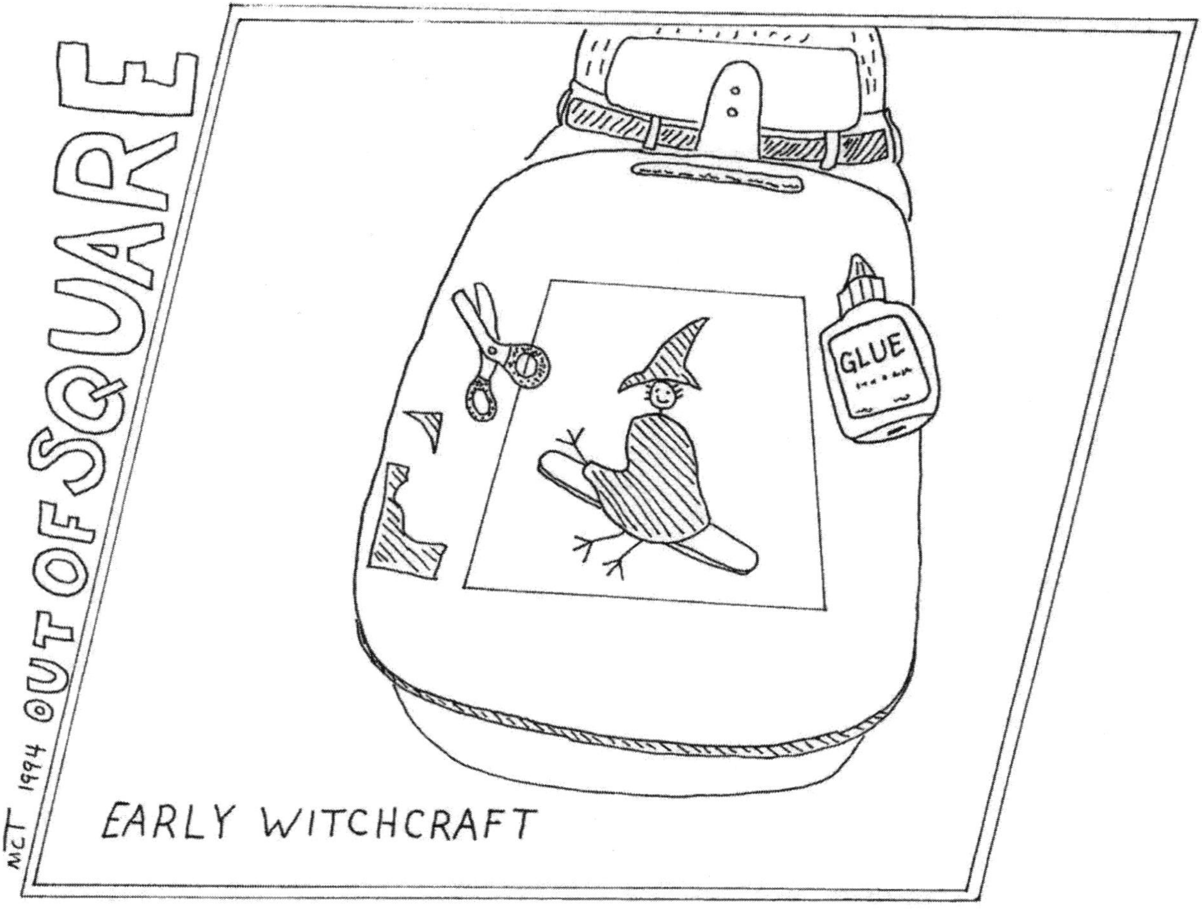
OUT OF SQUARE
©1994
MCT
GLUE

EARLY WITCHCRAFT

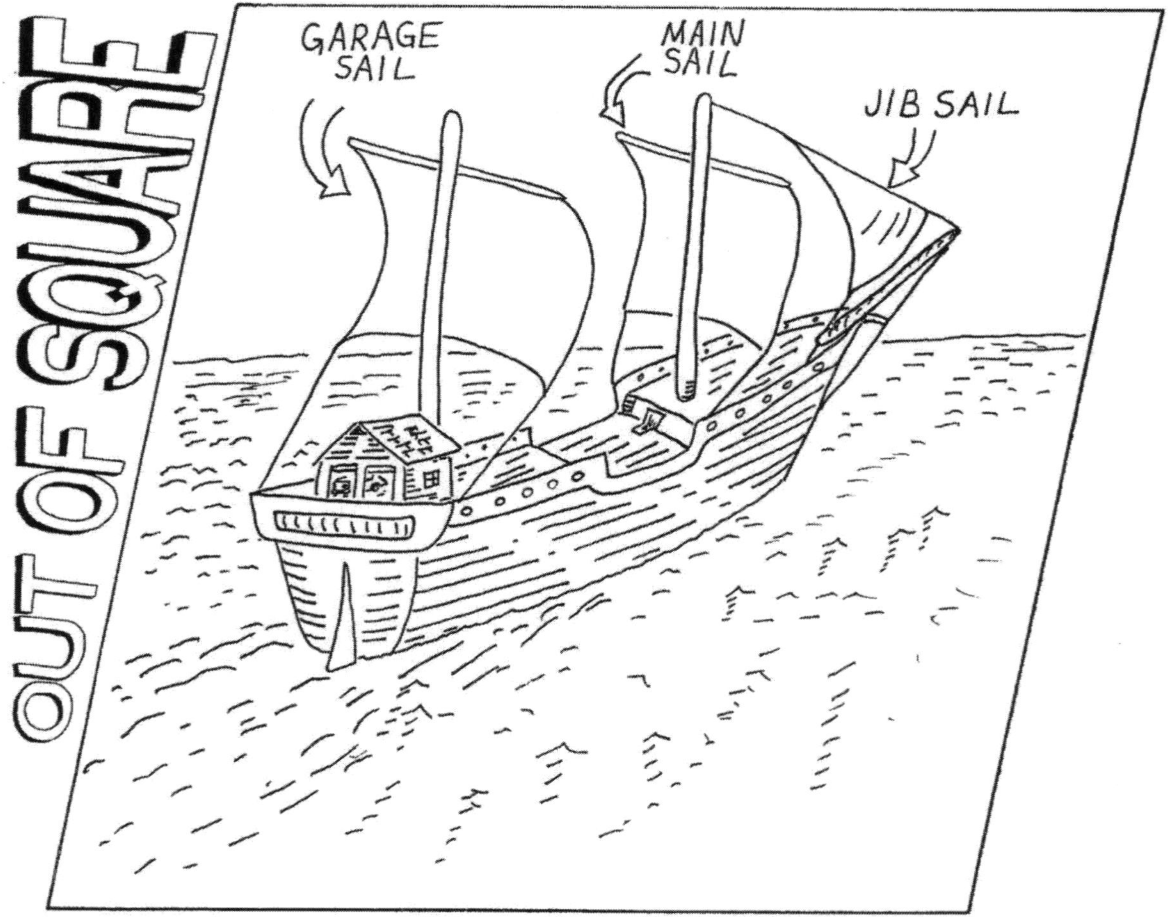
OUT OF SQUARE
GARAGE SAIL
MAIN SAIL
JIB SAIL

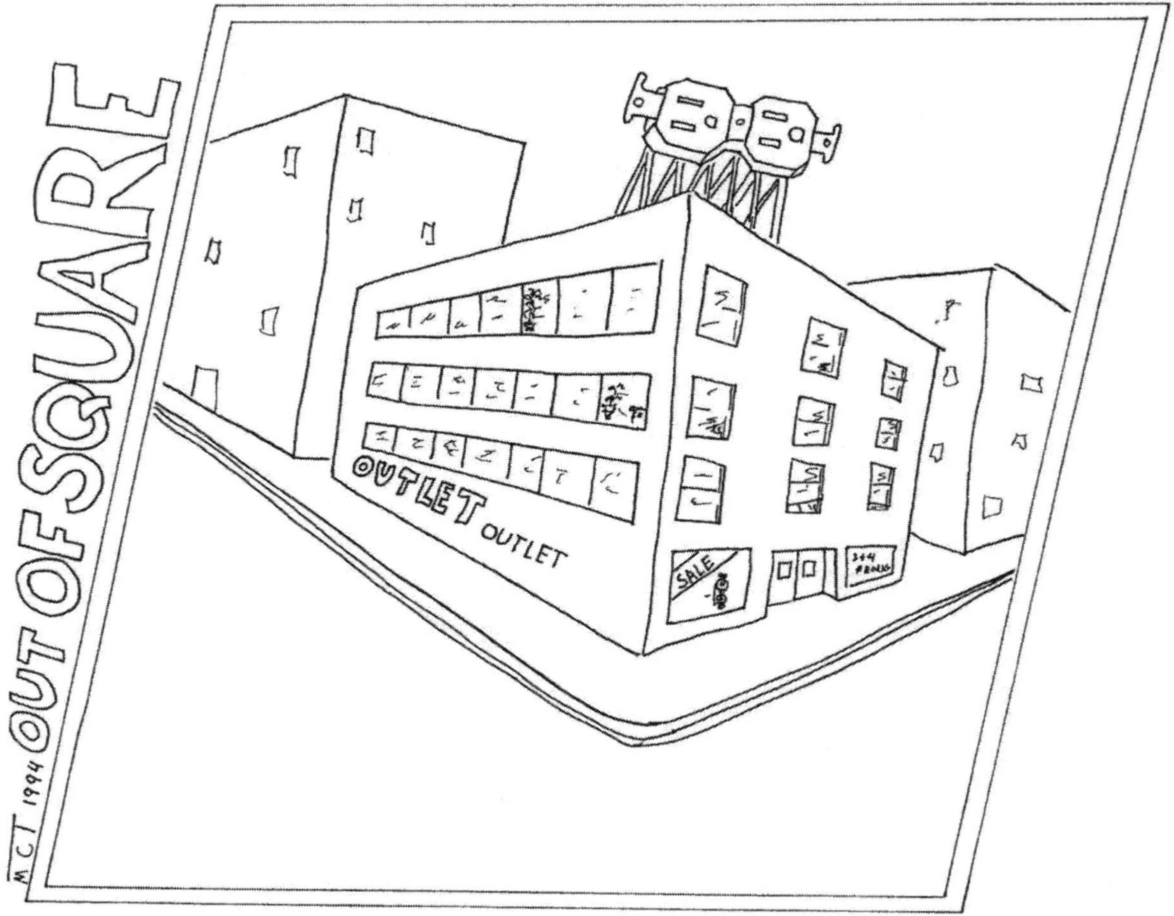
MCT 1994
OUT OF SQUARE
OUTLET
OUTLET
SALE

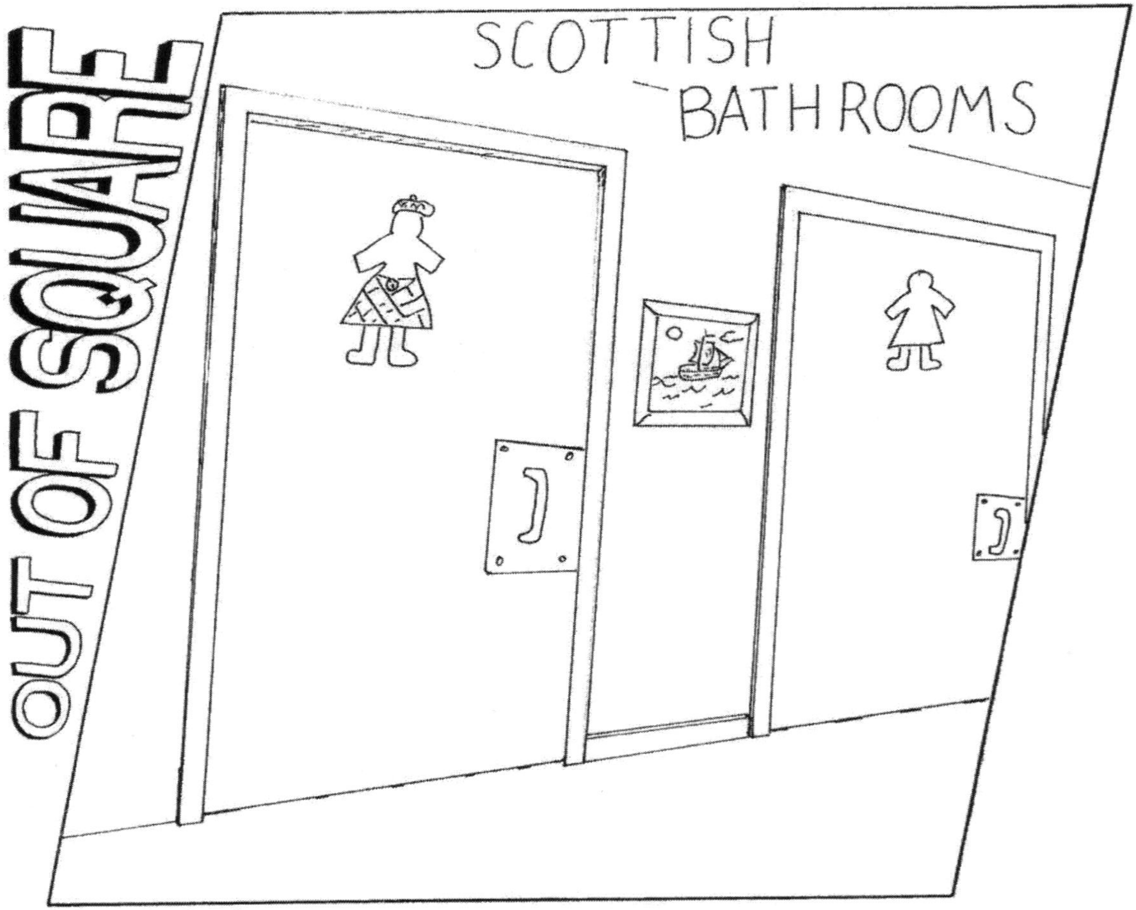
OUT OF SQUARE
SCOTTISH
BATHROOMS

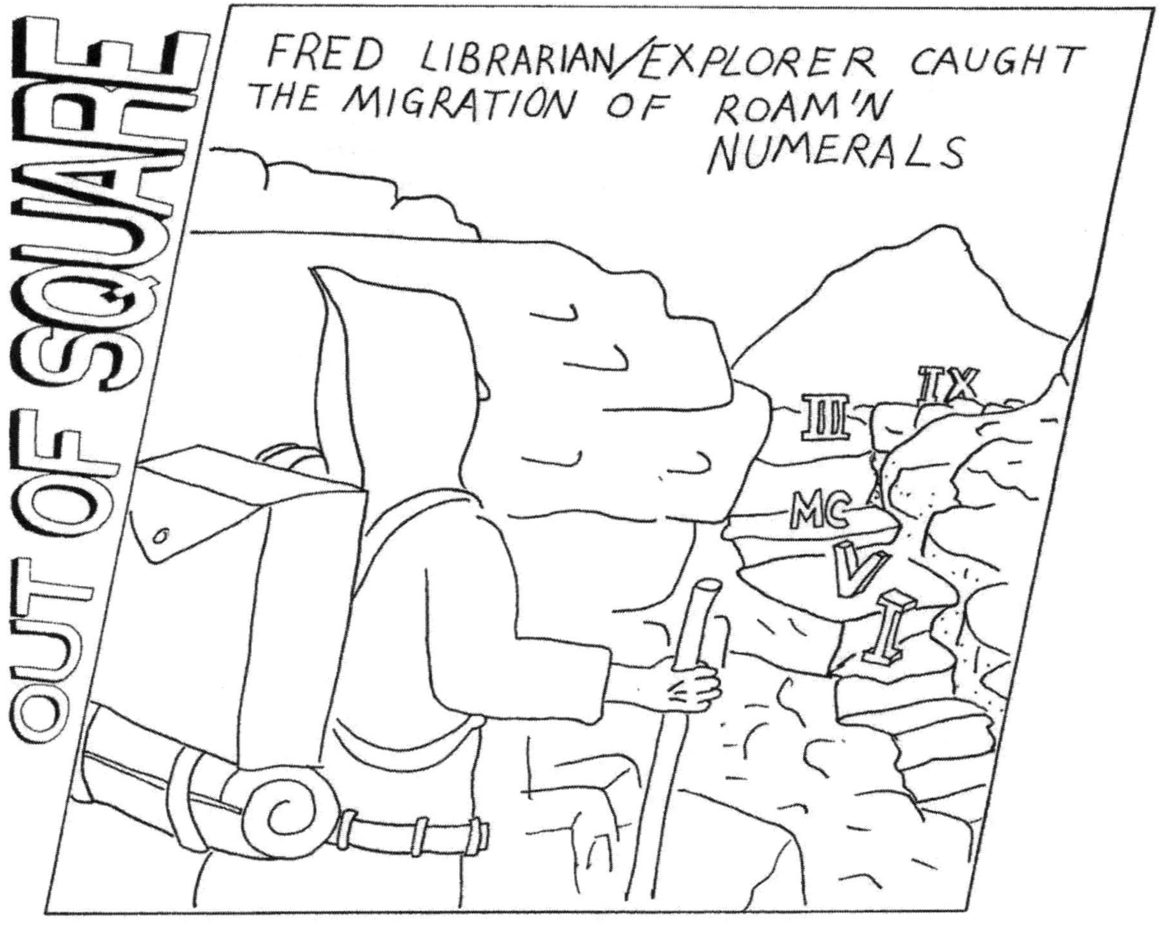
OUT OF SQUARE
FRED LIBRARIAN/EXPLORER CAUGHT THE MIGRATION OF ROAM'N NUMERALS
IX
III
MC
V
I

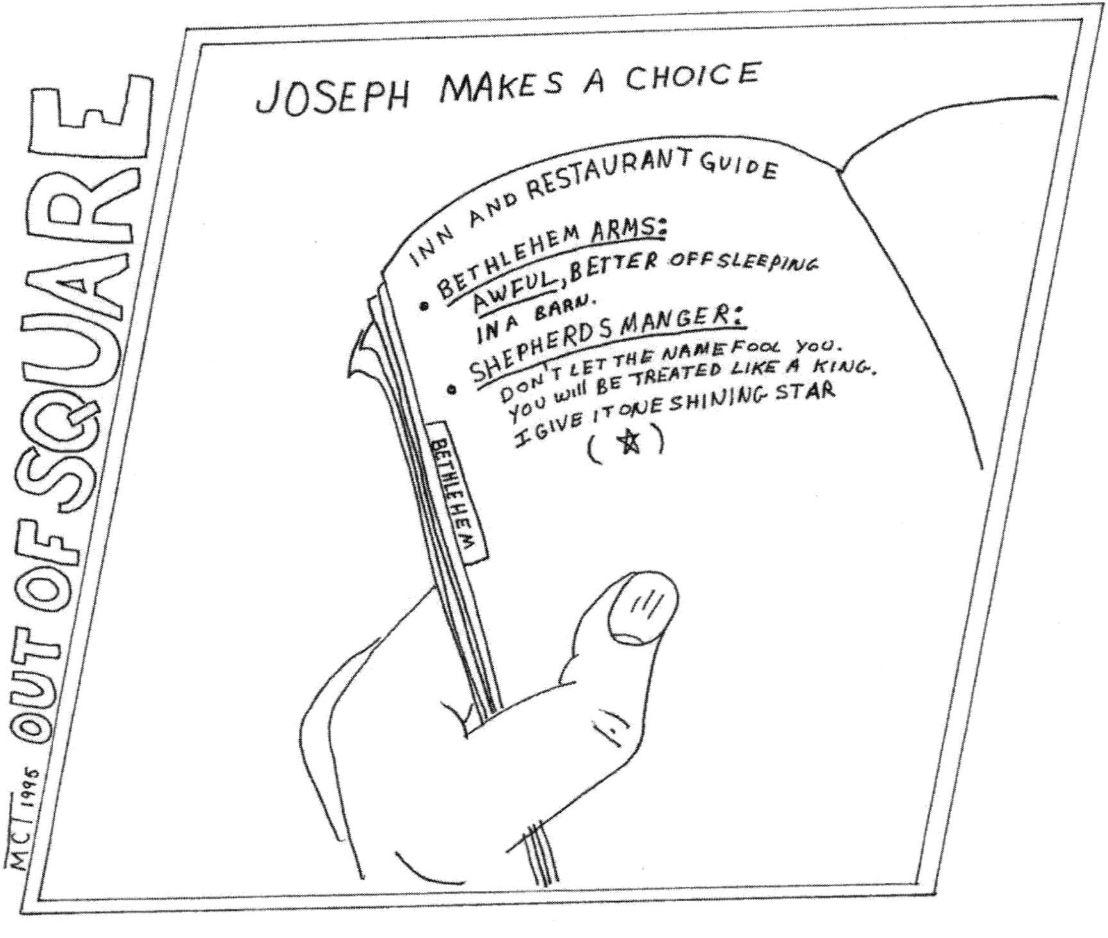
OUT OF SQUARE
MCT 1995
JOSEPH MAKES A CHOICE
INN AND RESTAURANT GUIDE
BETHLEHEM ARMS:
AWFUL, BETTER OFF SLEEPING IN A BARN.
SHEPHERDS MANGER:
DON'T LET THE NAME FOOL YOU. YOU will BE TREATED LIKE A KING. I GIVE IT ONE SHINING STAR
(☆)
BETHLEHEM

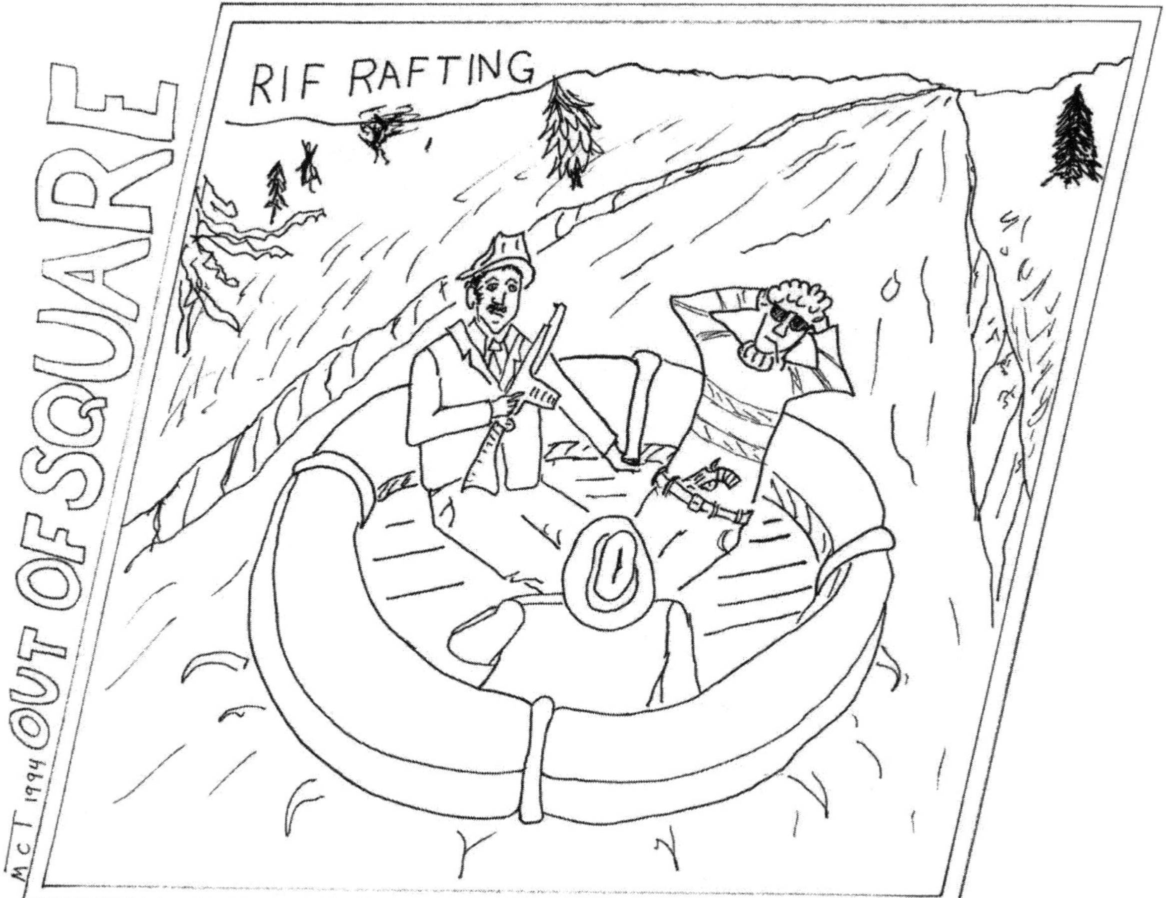
OUT OF SQUARE
McT 1994
RIF RAFTING

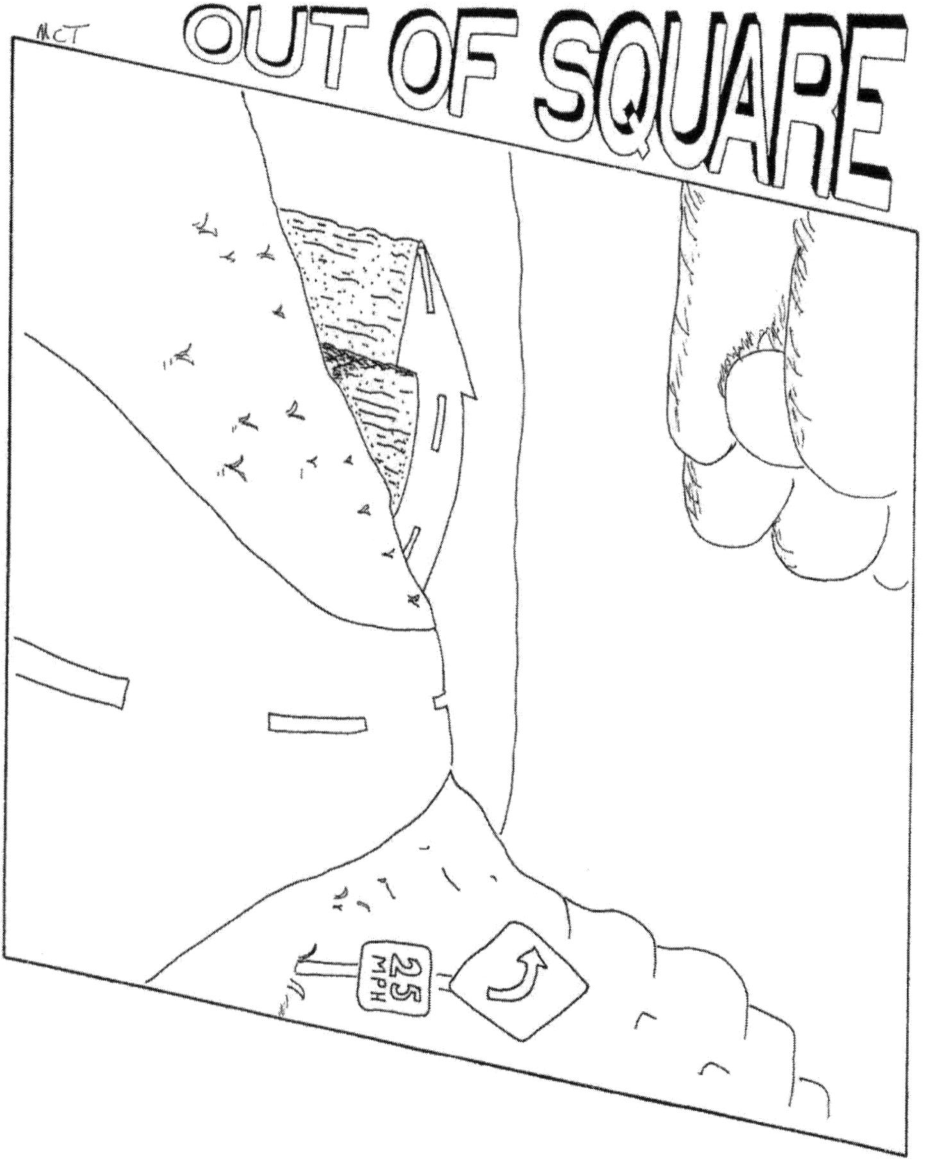
MCT
OUT OF SQUARE
25
MPH

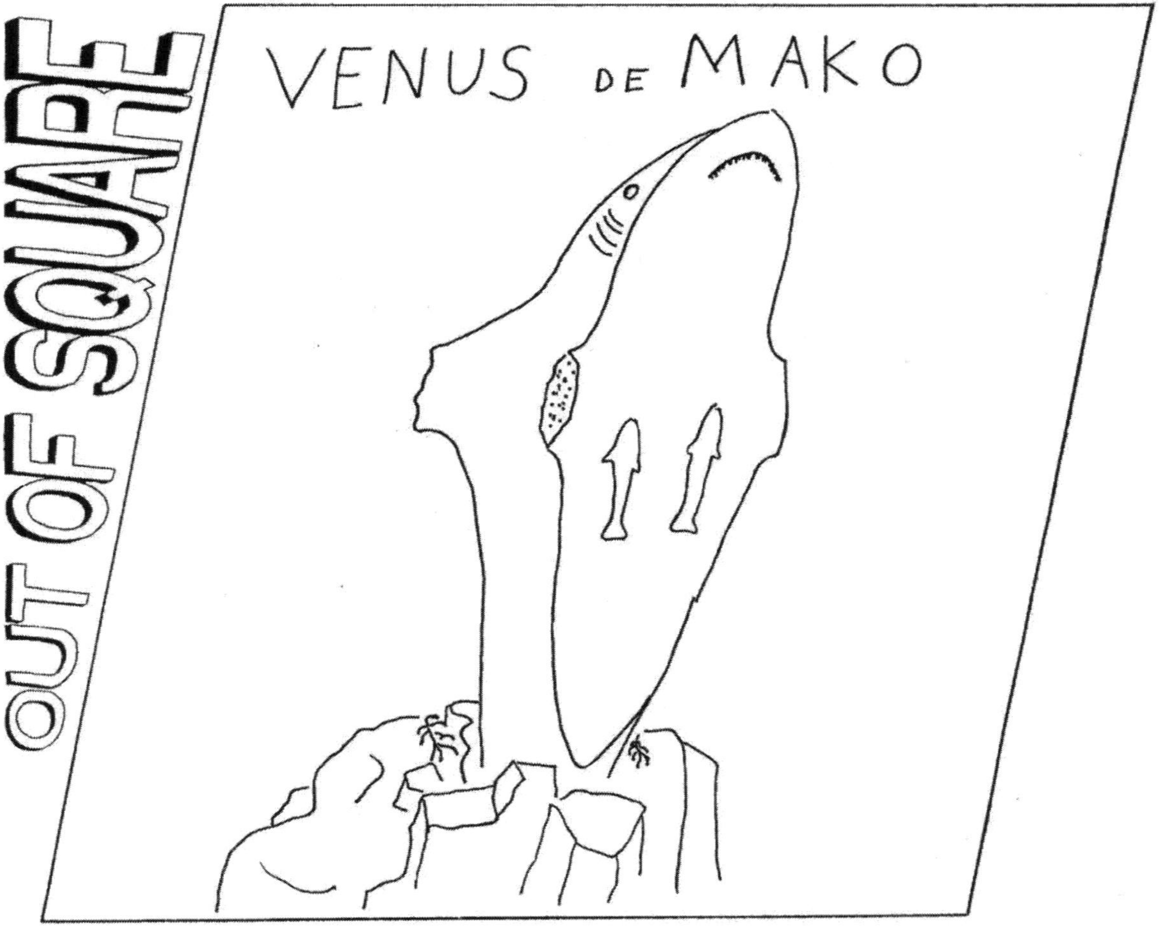
OUT OF SQUARE
VENUS DE MAKO

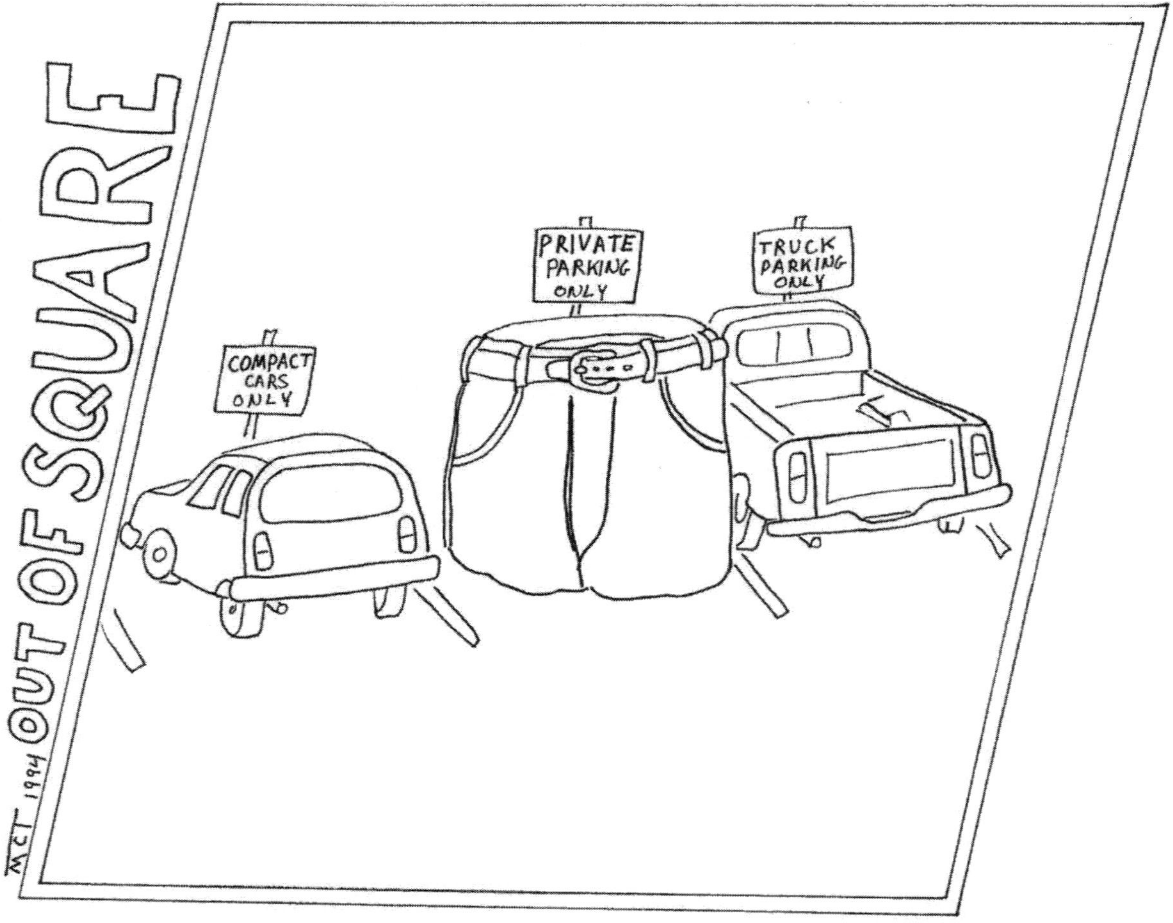
OUT OF SQUARE
MCT 1994
COMPACT CARS ONLY
PRIVATE PARKING ONLY
TRUCK PARKING ONLY

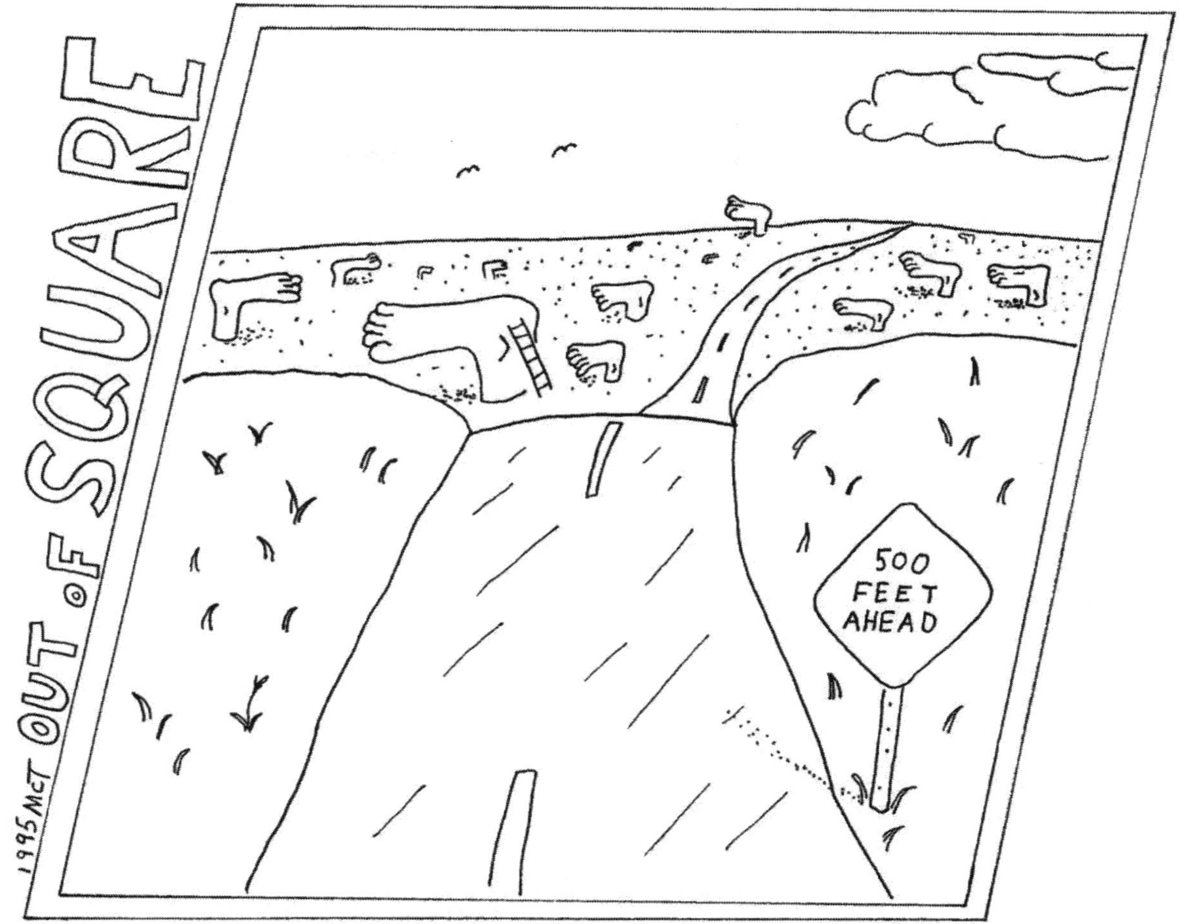
OUT OF SQUARE
1995 MCT
500 FEET AHEAD

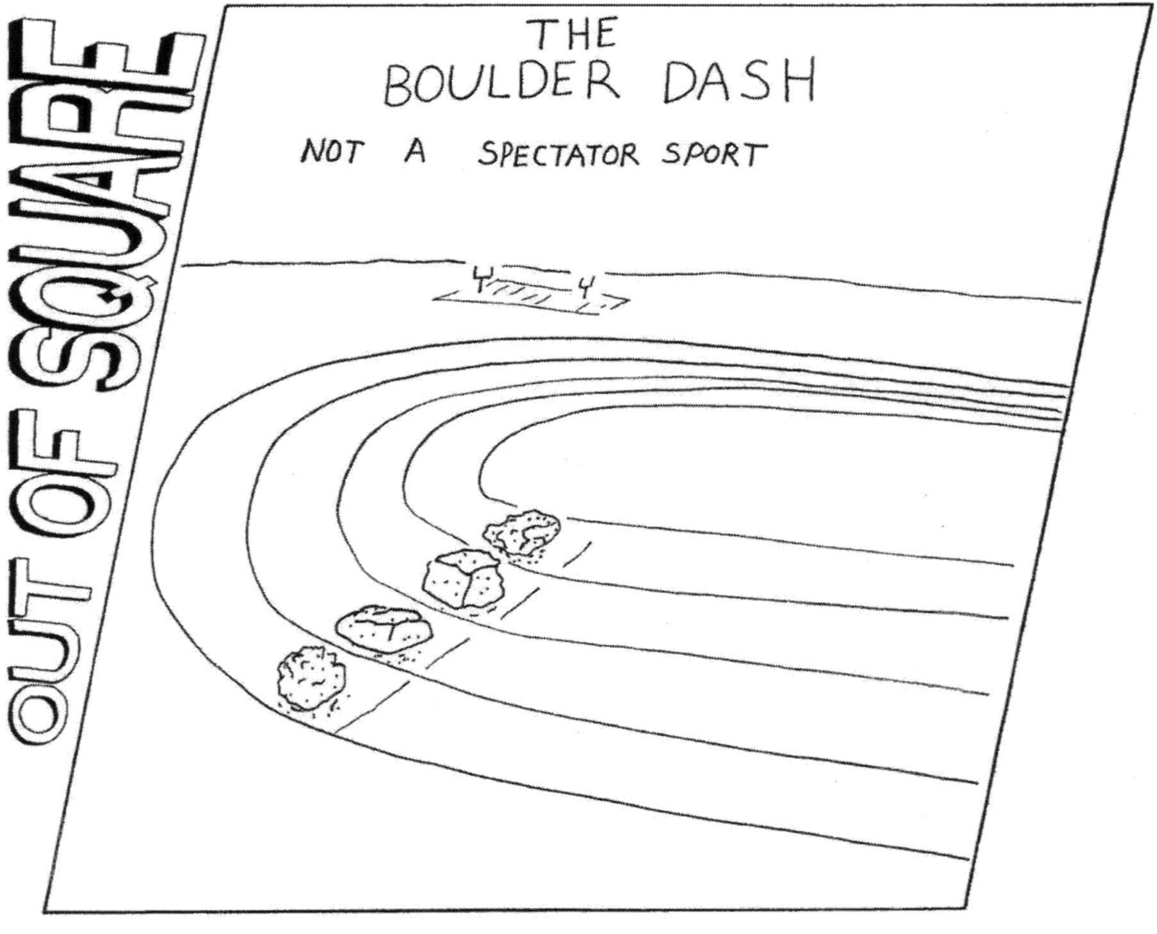
OUT OF SQUARE
THE
BOULDER DASH
NOT A SPECTATOR SPORT

OUT OF SQUARE

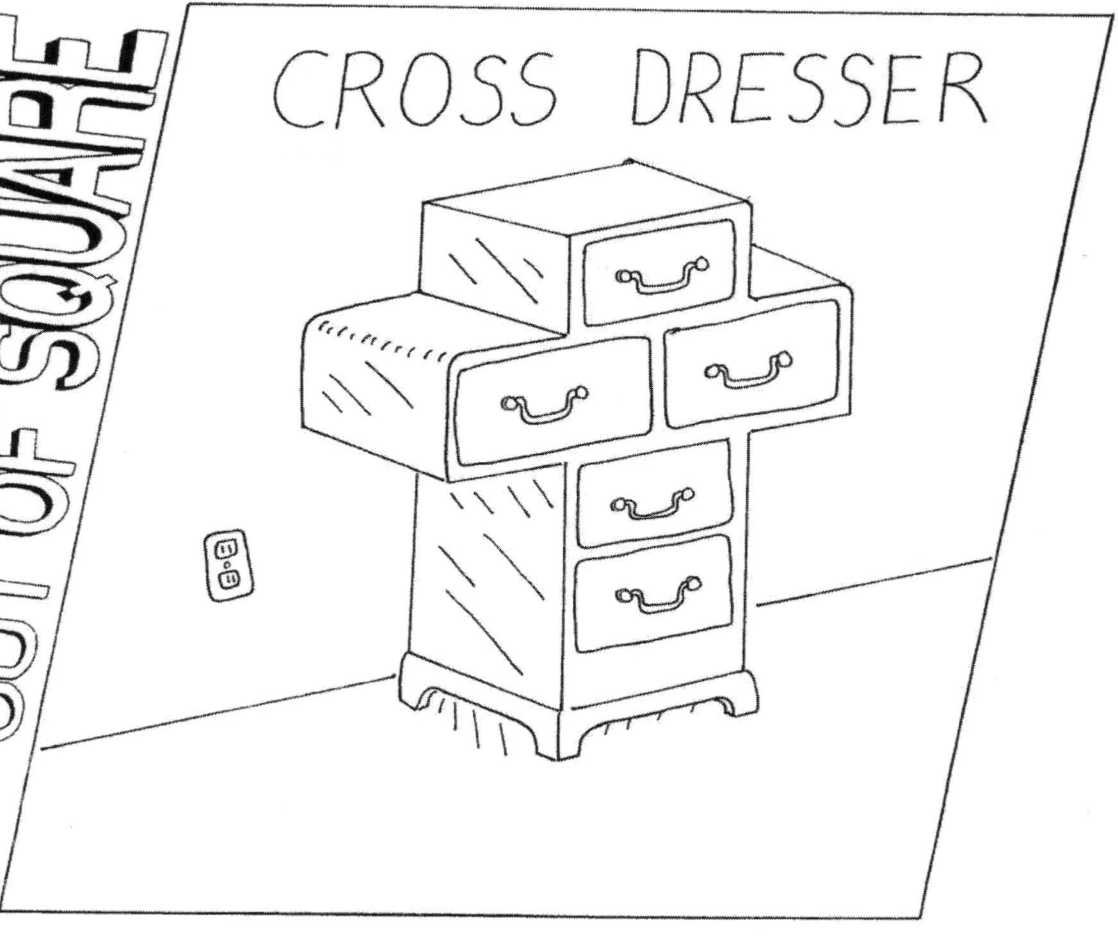
CROSS DRESSER

OUT OF SQUARE

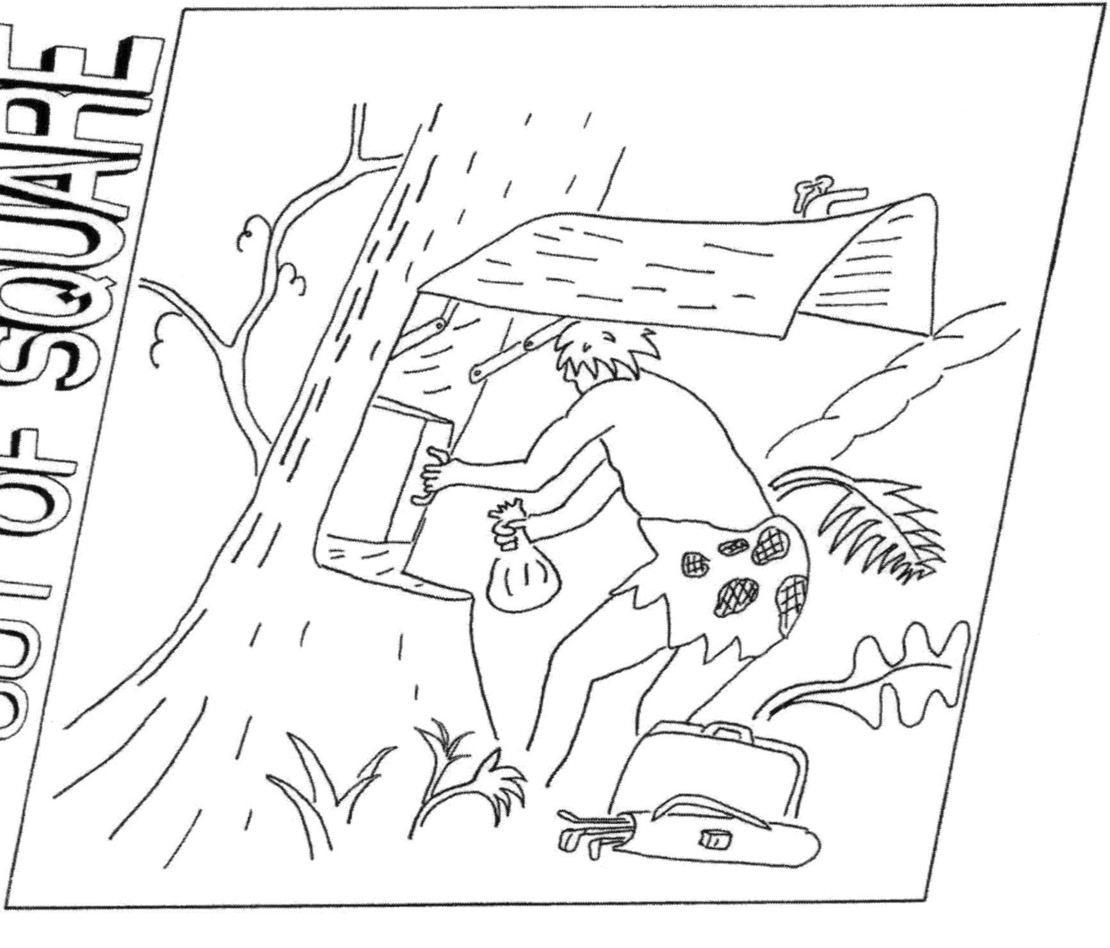

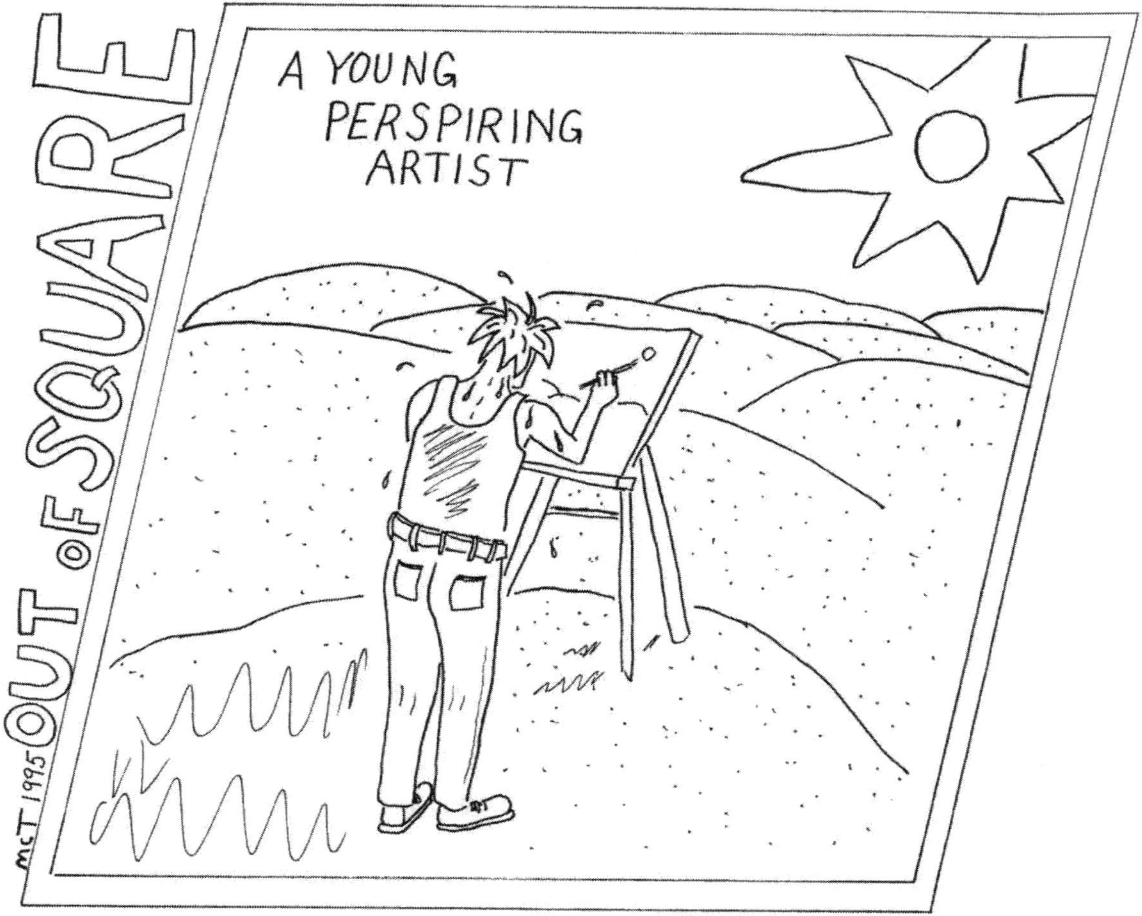
OUT OF SQUARE
McT 1995
A YOUNG PERSPIRING ARTIST

8778354R0

Made in the USA
Charleston, SC
13 July 2011